Like a Mother

Like a Mother

BANISH GUILT, BLAZE YOUR TRAIL, AND BREAK THE RULES TO CREATE A LIFE YOU LOVE

Bethany Braun-Silva

FIRST EDITION

Like a Mother

Banish Guilt, Blaze Your Trail, and Break the Rules
to Create a Life You Love

Printed in the United States of America

First Edition

ISBN 9798218196257 paperback
ISBN 9798218196264 ebook
Library of Congress Control Number: 2023907342

Cover and Interior Design by:
Chris Treccani

Cover Artwork by:
Nicole Wilson

Created with the Book to Millions® Method

DEDICATION

For my mother, and her mother, and you and your mother.

CONTENTS

FOREWORD

To know Bethany is to *adore* her. She's a champion of others, a girl's girl with a quiet way of making you feel seen when you need it the most. She's the first to reach out and ask you if you need help, and she means it. I guess it should be no surprise that Bethany has written a book with the purpose of lifting us all up.

As a working mom of two young kids, I found myself nodding, smiling, and crying—all while wondering if Bethany was in my literal head when she was writing *Like A Mother*.

Essentially, *all* the feels.

I'm not trying to tell anyone how they should read this book, but what I suggest is to read it all the way through, then keep it close. Whenever you need a pep talk, a virtual hug, to feel like you're not alone in this parenting journey, or simply need some inspiration . . . pick it back up and read the chapter you need in the moment. That's what I plan to do.

With that said, it's about time this forever cheerleader gets her time to shine!

Bethany . . . You deserve it all and more, Mama! Thank you for your friendship. Thank you for always highlighting the best in everyone. And thank you for this beautiful book.

XOXO Joelle

—Joelle Garguilo

New York–based reporter, spreader of good news, and mother

PREFACE

Before we dive into the words and message of this book, let's take a musical journey, shall we? I invite you to download and play one of my favorite songs as a preface to this book, "I'll Kill You If You Don't Come Back," written by James Steinman and performed by the late, great Meat Loaf…RIP. About four minutes into the six-minute song, Meat Loaf starts singing about different types of girls, and it got me thinking about what a dichotomy it is to be a woman.

Gorgeous and fierce. Strong and scared. Brave and guilt-ridden. Tired and determined.

No, this isn't a poor attempt at an Alanis knock-off; this is real life. This Meat Loaf song is one of my favorites because we've all been one of these girls at some point. To me, these lyrics represent the expectations placed on us, consciously or unconsciously, by ourselves or others. Somewhere along the way, if you are a woman, you've probably been told how to act, what to be, and, more likely, what not to be.

I have my own style. There's an edge to the way that I communicate as a New Yorker. I'm funny and not judgmental. When I was younger, I was sometimes uncomfortable with these traits. Now, I own them!

What do you love about yourself? My goal in writing this book is for you to embrace the traits you've developed, the growth you've experienced, the person you've become. It's for you to love yourself first, forge your own path, create your own rules, and blaze your own trail—unapologetically.

INTRODUCTION

For the longest time, life has gone in order.

"First comes love, then comes marriage, then comes the baby in the baby carriage."

In 2017, I had an idea for a book. I was just starting to come out of the haze of raising kids long enough to get inspired. I started thinking about the unwritten rules of life—especially the rules taught to girls—and I kept coming back to the nursery rhyme: "First comes love, then comes marriage, then comes the baby in the baby carriage."

It played in my head, over and over—probably because I felt like I messed it up. It wasn't

supposed to be like this.

It's supposed to be: Love first. Marriage second. Baby third.

Here I was, two kids deep, unmarried, and not even sure I knew what love meant.

I was creating a career from the ground up, and I was full of doubts and insecurities. I was raising my two boys and feeling unsteady every step of the way. My relationship with their father? Well, let's just say I have enough content to fill a second book.

But here's what I knew for sure: I. HAD. MYSELF.

In the midst of the haze and throughout my 30-plus years of life, I had never let myself down *too* badly, and I sure as shit wasn't going to start now. Becoming a mother, experiencing the love I had for my son—woke up something inside me.

There's a fierceness that's born inside a mother in tandem with welcoming her children. I've seen it in mothers I know (my own included)—the fierce desire to love, protect, and nurture— it all gets fired up when we have our kids.

What if we could redirect that fierceness toward ourselves? What if all the mothers, who love and nurture and protect others so fiercely, started treating themselves the same way? What would the world look like?

Imagine all the mothers of the world mothering themselves. Loving themselves unconditionally. Protecting themselves from dangerous and unwanted situations. Nurturing themselves when they are sad or disappointed. Or better yet, encouraging themselves to try again after disappointment and to explore new passions.

What if we started treating ourselves *like a mother*?

And that's where the idea for this book was born. As I looked back on the life I had carved out for myself as a girl who grew up in New York City, as a 26-year-old who became a mother before she was ready (what does that really mean anyway?), as a professional who charged her way up the ladder without any real education to back it up—I knew that I wanted to share my story as a way to encourage women to break the rules, make their own, and answer only to themselves. I wanted to inspire women to go out into the world like a mother: Loving and fierce, with a new set of rules to play by.

But what happens when your rules, dreams, and hard work are shattered by a worldwide pandemic? The pandemic was devastating, especially for women. Weren't we already doing enough—raising kids, working hard to earn less, making sacrifice after sacrifice? The pandemic knocked over 4 million women out of the workforce.[1]

Women take on more of the household responsibilities and mental load of parenthood than their male counterparts. The pandemic came as a slap in the face, forcing us to leave jobs, businesses, and passions—it quite literally broke us.

But now, nearly three years after the pandemic started, women are reemerging. They are going back to work, starting their own businesses, and bringing their family life back under control. But we can't return to how things were before, to how things *weren't* working.

It's time for women to reemerge with new rules. Rules we create for ourselves. Rules that let us live our lives the way that works best for us. Our lives. Our rules.

This book presents my personal experience and advice along with the personal experience and advice of successful women I admire, with the goal of helping *you* live your best life in exactly the way you want. But please, take what you want and leave what you don't. The main point of this book is to inspire you to write a few new rules of your own.

If you're like me and you tend to jump to the end of books, you'll be happy to see what waits for you there . . . although this isn't a work of fiction, and there's no surprise ending. There are, however, guided prompts to help you record your thoughts if you feel inspired to do so. More on that below.

The book is divided into three parts:

1. Let's Talk about Self, Baby!
2. Friends, Lovers, and Others
3. Work and Ambition

For each of the areas covered—self, relationships, and work—we'll dive into how you can banish guilt, blaze your trail, and create a life you love.

Here are the features you'll find in each chapter:

1. Each chapter begins with an **Old Rule** and a **New Rule**. The old rule represents something we were taught, something we unconsciously believed. The new rule represents how we can shift the old rule into something that works for us today.
2. In each chapter's **Spotlight**, I'll introduce you to a woman I've conversed with or interviewed on my podcast, *The Breakdown with Bethany*. We'll meet nine women in all, and all of them are mothers. My podcast unleashes my passion for connecting with other women and having a shared voice when it comes to motherhood, work, ambition, and relationships. I launched the show so I could highlight women I admire, respect, and aspire to be by sharing their passions and tips for success. Together, we're amplifying each other's voices and creating a supportive community.
3. The **Rule Breaker** is a woman in the public eye who has defied society's expectations, is fierce in her love for herself, and represents the idea of living life on her own terms.
4. **Recognize, Reframe, Reconnect**—or the 3Rs, as I call them—is a simple strategy I use to practice self-love and encourage myself when I'm feeling down, stressed, or overwhelmed. In these sections, I'll teach you how to recognize, reframe, and reconnect when you find yourself in various scenarios that aren't serving you.

5. **Bethany's Chapter Breakdown** is a one-sentence wrap-up of what each chapter is about. The breakdown is meant to motivate you to action.

The last chapter is for you. Start setting your own rules and expectations. To learn how to talk to yourself like your own best friend. To be confident in the choices you make regarding your career and family. To stop looking outward for reassurance—to be bold enough and strong enough to make choices for yourself. To lose your fear of loving yourself first. To discover self-love, put that into your relationships, and then return to self-love in order to pursue your dreams and ambitions.

Let's get started.

Part 1:

Let's Talk About Self, Baby!

"Love yourself first, and everything else falls into line. You really have to love yourself to get anything done in this world."

-Lucille Ball

Let's talk about *you*.

For some women, talking about themselves is easy. They can go on and on about their family life and relationships, their thoughts, feelings, emotions, and kids. But for some of us, talking about ourselves is tough. And consequently, loving ourselves—giving ourselves time, space, and grace—is even harder.

Women are the ultimate cheerleaders. We hype up our girlfriends with endless inspiration, telling them things like:

"You got this." "You're phenomenal."

"You're way too good for that loser."

The energy we put into our relationships—romantic and platonic—seems to be never-ending.

We have all the time in the world to support others. But what if we treated ourselves like we treat our BFFs? My girlfriends are some of the most important people in my life. Friendships, whether forged decades ago or months ago, have catapulted me into professional success and cradled me during romantic rock bottoms.

But even if you're as lucky as I've been with female friendships, it's ultimately not enough.

Your girlfriends can't make you break up with an abusive loser (try as they may). They can't make you advocate for the promotion you deserve (although on more than one occasion, I've used a girlfriend as a job "reference"). And as much as they tell you how amazing and worthy you are, you won't actually believe it until you start telling *yourself* those things. It all comes from within!

CHAPTER 1:

Self-Love

"People feel uncomfortable around women who don't hate themselves, but that's their issue, not yours."

-Mindy Kaling

Old Rule: The best women don't make much noise. They put everyone else first.
New Rule: Put yourself first unapologetically, and be loud about it.

It all begins with love.

Chances are, you came into this world as a product of love. If you didn't, love was most likely the first emotion you felt. You probably loved looking at yourself in the mirror as a baby and exclaimed with joy when you grew an inch or two as a child.

But somewhere along the way—maybe sooner rather than later—you learned not to love yourself. You were told, either directly or indirectly, that you weren't worthy. Thus began your journey outward. I'm here to help guide you back to yourself—back to love.

One of my earliest memories is of my mother telling me, "Thoughts are things. What you
think, you will become."

She said this to me almost every day of my childhood, especially when I said something negative about myself. This mantra was so deeply ingrained in me that even to this day, I find myself repeating, "What you think, you will become," like a broken record. My mother believed so much in the power of positive thinking that just hearing me say something negative about myself would send her into an inspirational monologue.

Brooklyn-born and Queens-raised, she once told me, "If you don't stop saying all that bad
shit about yourself, I'm gonna come over there and knock your fuckin' head off."

Well, I still have my head, despite saying not-so-nice things about myself every now and then. But we can't possibly get through our lives, raise our kids, and excel at our careers if we don't love ourselves.

For some of us, the idea of loving ourselves is too much. If you've believed for a long time that you're unworthy, it'll definitely take more than me telling you that you're deserving of self-love to break through that belief.

We don't want to take up space. Somewhere along the line, women are told that being smaller is better—smaller personalities, smaller dress sizes, smaller everything. We constantly want to lose weight. We try to shrink ourselves to fit in when we should be taking up more space—being seen but not heard, being agreeable.

How do we start to love ourselves?

My mother recently dropped another jewel on me. I was feeling overwhelmed about buying a home, making enough money, and excelling in my career. I said something about being overwhelmed by finances—which is a legitimate reason to freak out—and followed up by resolving to do four or five things to fix the problem that weren't aligned with my current path.

My mother responded, "Don't create a solution when you don't even know if there is a

problem."

I do this often—worry for no reason. I try to get ahead of problems by coming up with solutions that don't serve me or make me happy. In this instance, my mother stopped me dead in my tracks. There wasn't a problem; I was creating one out of my own fear and anxiety.

Our thoughts create our reality. I certainly don't want my reality to be filled with fear and anxiety; I want it to be filled with love. At that moment, all the fear and worry I was feeling was actually the *opposite* of loving myself. I felt undeserving of the good things that were happening to me. I was focused on a problem that didn't exist, and my response was a form of self-sabotage.

This interaction with my mother triggered memories of countless times when she picked me up when I was down, helping me shift to a positive mindset. That's what mothers *do*— they care for their children in almost otherworldly ways. I care for my kids this way, and the mothers I know do the same for their kids. To love like a mother means to love without fail, to see beyond the negative and nasty, and to see people for who they are at their core.

That was the inspiration for the title of this book. I know my mother loves me big-time, with a capital "L." But at times, I and my mother and probably you, too—we find it so hard to love ourselves. We need to start thinking about the ways we've seen mothers love their children. If you've experienced that love for yourself, you know what it means to love *like a mother*.

Start turning that love toward yourself. Start loving yourself *like a mother*—unconditionally, in spite of your faults and failures.

Good things happen all the time, so why not to me? Why not you? The good things we want and deserve come to us when we love ourselves unapologetically. (Right, Mom?)

Spotlight: Dr. Whitney Casares

Meet Dr. Whitney Casares, renowned private-practice pediatrician, two-time American Academy of Pediatrics author and spokesperson, and mom to two young girls in Portland, Oregon.

Dr. Whitney's mission, although she's a pediatrician, is to help mothers through the first few months after giving birth—and that resonates strongly with me. I've guested on her podcast, and she's guested on mine. If you're a mom—new or experienced—I highly recommend checking out modernmommydoc.com to see what Dr. Whitney is all about and for some helpful resources. Here's a bit of our conversation on *The Breakdown with Bethany* on the importance of self-care.

Bethany: What's something you're struggling with? Because you wrote an amazing book, you're a mom of two, and you're a pediatrician. From the outside looking in, it seems like "She's got it together."

Whitney: That's a good question. And here's the thing. If I can't be vulnerable with people, then I have nothing to give. I really think that. Brene

Brown says that vulnerability is the biggest gift we can give ourselves and other people.

In my book, I talk a lot about my relationship with my husband and about struggles we went through early on. My husband is a very social person, and my oldest daughter McKenna—who I wrote a ton about in the book—she is, too. And Covid took a toll on these exuberant people who are super smart and who could not be duped by niceties like saying, "It's all going to be fine. It's going to be good. Don't worry. Just hold on." Both of them were like, "This is horrible. The world's ending. Let's just call it."

It's hard because I don't always want to be the bubbly one. I don't always want to carry the torch for our family. Sometimes I need respite. Sometimes I need someone taking care of *me*. And this year, I feel like I've been holding the family together. So, now that things are opening up a bit, I have to go to my exercise class with other people. I have to take time to listen to the music that I love. I have to sit outside on the porch and put on headphones and read a book or listen to a podcast that I love.

I think the struggle has just been making sure that I continue to show up for myself at a time when those around me—my patients, my partner, my kids—have needed so much from me. I've had to remember that if I don't have myself, I have nothing to give.

Bethany: We talk a lot about self-care, but lately, I feel like it's become a buzzword. I want to know how moms can advocate for themselves, for self-care, even within their own families. Because obviously, we all need it, but it's so hard to actually do it.

Whitney: I think it comes down to being aware of what makes you feel the most alive and awake. Those are the things that really care for your soul. For me, music is the thing that always makes me feel the most alive and awake. So, self-care for me, pre-Covid, might be going to a concert with my husband and being in that moment with him and connected. That's self-care.

I also love really good food. Self-care could be going out to dinner with a girlfriend. I love movement. Self-care could be, sitting in my basement doing yoga—not to fit into a size zero but to be able to say, "Oh my gosh, that stretch feels so good on my body." Those are the things that I think of when I'm considering what I would do on a perfect day if I had no obligations, no kids, no husband. Those are the things I always come back to, the things I need to integrate into my life.

In my book, I mention that it's not enough to say these things—you have to go *do* them sometimes. I try to be a little bit formulaic about it. You need to fill your cup a little bit every day. Practice self-care, find yourself, be

> awake, be alive, return to your passion, to what brings you joy. Do *that,* as opposed to letting your cup drain completely—then you've got to pour in a whole gallon, and it's way too much.
>
> There's almost a sort of bulimic or yo-yo thing that happens with moms, where we deprive ourselves, self-sacrifice, give everything to our kids and our jobs, and then we're empty and miserable. Then we do something to cope, and our coping mechanisms are maybe not as healthy. We overeat or drink too much alcohol or binge watch Netflix for three days in a row. Or we may explode at our kids and say, "I've had it. I need to get out of here." The key for me is to have micro-doses of self-care every day. And I practice that by doing five minutes a day of some type of quiet time alone, like a guided meditation. I'm horrible at thinking of what I should meditate about, so I do guided meditations.

To hear more of our interview, listen to Episode #12 of *The Breakdown with Bethany.*

Meet the Rule Breaker: Mindy Kaling

Mindy Kaling is one of my favorite actresses/creators/directors/writers. She's unapologetically herself, and I've been fortunate enough to have the opportunity to interview her.

I love Mindy's strength and personality. By being herself, she gives us permission to be ourselves. She doesn't look or talk according to the norms we're used to. She's broken through and risen to the top to become an icon of what it means to be a woman, a mother, and a creator.

Here's what Mindy had to say about high standards and not apologizing in our interview.

> I have really high standards for myself, professionally and personally. And I see pictures of other people doing really fun things—like, they created like an obstacle course for their kids in the backyard—and I feel so guilty or jealous that I didn't think of that. Meanwhile, my daughter's watching *The Grinch* for the 90th time on TV. And I didn't have the creativity and the patience to build an obstacle course with her. I'm not the mom that does that.
>
> I think what I have decided to come to terms with in 2020 is that I'm going to ignore those feelings of jealousy and be like, 'This is a short time in the grand scheme of her childhood, and if she watched a little bit too much TV during this past ten months (and for the next couple of months), that's okay.'
>
> She's eventually going to go back to school, and maybe she didn't get to have an amazing obstacle course in the backyard. Or maybe I didn't feel like doing another craft project with her because it was just too messy in the kitchen. I didn't want to deal with the cleanup. It's going to be okay. I wasn't raised with any of that stuff, and I turned out pretty happy and successful. Just allowing myself to not have those feelings—or to not be affected by those feelings—is huge for me.

To hear more of our interview, listen to Episode #1 of *The Breakdown with Bethany.*

Tips to Implement Right Now

How can we start practicing self-love? How can we start showing up for ourselves in small ways (and then hopefully in bigger ways)?

Starting your self-love journey can be as simple as practicing gratitude for yourself, your body, and your thoughts.

Or, it can be as big as setting a long-overdue boundary, forgiving someone who hurt you, forgiving yourself, quitting a job, applying for a new job, leaving a relationship, or starting a business.

Here are three tips you can implement right now:

1. Begin to rely on validation from yourself rather than from others.
2. Say "No" to what no longer feels good.
3. Don't be so hard on yourself—remember, you're human!

Recognize	**Reframe**	**Reconnect**
Recognize when you're not loving yourself. If you're angry, frustrated, or not feeling in alignment with yourself-that should alert you that you're not loving yourself.	We think it's so hard to get out of a funk. But when you replace the negativity and frustration you're feeling with new language, you'll see how quickly your attitude shifts.	You can reconnect with yourself by setting intentions. An intention for your day can be something like, "Today, I'm going to take it slow and check in with myself to make sure I'm in alignment with my thoughts and feelings."

Bethany's Chapter Breakdown

Treat yourself like you are your own best friend.

CHAPTER 2:

Self-Talk

"This confidence is not something that happens overnight. I have been working on it for a long time. I look in the mirror and do affirmations: 'You are bold. You are brilliant. You are beautiful.' If my lower pooch is really popping out that day, I look at it and say, 'Pooch, you are cute!'"

-Ashley Graham

Old Rule: Talking to yourself is weird and will make you seem crazy.
New Rule: You are your own best friend, so start talking to yourself like it.

When I was a little girl, I spent a lot of time by myself. That's the fate of an only child, especially one with two working parents. When you're alone, you talk to yourself. You create imaginary scenarios. You get to know yourself, your likes, dislikes, and triggers, your deep thoughts and fears.

As an adult, I recognize what was happening as I spent all that time alone as a child. Spending all that time alone, I unconsciously started to strengthen my relationship with myself. Sometimes I would talk to myself to curb my loneliness—just talking to myself like I was my own best friend. As I grew older, the talk shifted from positive, self-affirming conversations to hateful ones.

This is the case for many girls as they grow into their teenage years—the conversations they have with themselves tend to shift to self-doubt, self-hatred, body image issues, and a lack of confidence. Perhaps we can blame society, our parents or friends, or the media.

Regardless, it's something that many—if not all—of us go through.

When our self-talk shifts from positive to negative as we enter our teenage years, it's not our own voice telling us we're ugly, fat, too loud, too arrogant, or just too much. It's other voices that we're letting into our heads. When we talk to ourselves in a negative way, it's rarely because those thoughts originate with us. It's more likely that someone said those things, explicitly or by implication. Then, consciously or unconsciously, we took those thoughts in.

We internalized them.

And it comes as no surprise that can be quite damaging. Negative self-talk can have a detrimental effect on a person's self-esteem and belief in their self-worth and abilities. The College of Cognitive Behavioural Therapies reports, "Negative self-talk will result in a vicious cycle and a negative self-fulfilling prophecy."[1]

We don't want self-fulfilling prophecies full of doubt and fear, so how do we break the cycle?

Usually, the first step is a long period of self-reflection. I recognize now that I set the foundation for this kind of reflection in my childhood, talking to myself, getting to know myself, and finding ways to self-soothe with words.

As I mentioned previously, women are quick to cheerlead for each other. We support, promote, and hype each other up, especially in rough times—after a betrayal or break ups, job loss, or even the loss of a child.

Our girlfriends are quick with their support—what would happen if we were that quick with support for ourselves if we could give ourselves everything we need? The simple act of talking to ourselves in a positive way helps us not only *feel* better but also *do* better, helping us create a better life for ourselves.

Many women have told me that they think the idea of being your own best friend sounds kind of silly. But then there's Mel Robbins encouraging people to literally high-five themselves in the mirror or Serena Kerrigan telling people to stand in front of the mirror and hype themselves up. Dozens, even hundreds, of high-achieving women cite positive self-talk as one of the keys to their success. So, it certainly *must* work. But it's not always that simple, is it?

I admit it does seem like a silly practice at first, but the rewards are incredible. We have to get over our self-consciousness, feeling like what we're doing is ridiculous. The way to do that is to start small. Recognize your negative thoughts when they pop up. Reframe them as positive thoughts. Then, reconnect to yourself and the world through new eyes.

In this first stage, we can enjoy our positive thoughts within our own heads until we're ready to speak them out loud. Start by talking to yourself in your head while looking in the mirror. Make small shifts when you catch yourself saying bad things about yourself, whether they're in your head or out loud. Small shifts from negative to positive can make a huge difference in your day and, eventually, in your life.

The best part is nobody has to know what you're doing. It's between you and your bestie— aka *yourself*.

Practice positive self-talk when you're feeling:

1. Self-doubt
2. Fear
3. Guilt
4. Alone
5. Invisible
6. Not good enough
7. Overwhelmed

Spotlight: Dr. Zabina Bhasin

Dr. Zabina Bhasin is a diversity and inclusion expert, entrepreneur, physician, and mom of two. She started a company called In KidZ that teaches children about global citizenship. If that isn't impressive enough, she's also an incredible thought leader when it comes to positivity, self-love, and the way we talk to ourselves.

Dr. Zee was an instant friend when we met. She's guested on my podcast, and we've hung out several times. For the book, I asked her a few questions about self-talk—her daily practice and how she exemplifies it for her kids. Here's what she had to say.

Bethany: You're a prime example of sharing positivity through your work and social media.

What's the impact of positive self-talk and affirmations, in your opinion?

Dr. Zee: The biggest impact of this is not for ourselves as adults; it's to show our children how positivity and affirmations can lift you up out of your own insecurities and make you a more secure, lovable, giving, and grateful person. When you say something enough times, even in your mind, you tend to believe it. So, if we repeat a lie many times, we're going to have a tendency to believe it.

The impact is speaking to yourself with positivity and affirmations of gratitude and love over and over again and showing our children how important it is to have this kind of positive self-talk.

Bethany: How do you instill these practices in your children?

Dr. Zee: It's not easy. Repetition is the most important part. I use meditation and affirmations, and self-talk all the time, and my daughter sees me do it all the time. She sees me and mimics me, and now my son does it as well. We instill this practice when they see us doing it and when we work with them to do it themselves. Twenty minutes a day—that's all you need.

Bethany: How can a mom get herself out of a negative self-talk spiral?

Dr. Zee: Using the same method I teach my kids. It comes from the books that I've read. But I always go back to *The Secret* by Rhonda Byrne.

There's one section that says that when you have a negative moment, and you have to turn it around quickly, think about things you love and care for—positive stuff—because that will really change your frame of mind.

If I'm in a negative spiral business-wise or in my personal life and I'm like, "Everything's not going right," I need to think immediately: What are the things I love? I love my kids. I love ice cream. I love dancing. I love music. I think about all those happy things. That's what I tell my kids. If my children are like, "I had a bad dream," or, "I'm having a bad thought," what do we do? My daughter loves unicorns. My son loves skateboards. That's what we think about. There's an immediate breakout from a negative spiral when you think about something positive, the thing that you love the most.

Bethany: Why does it matter how we talk to ourselves?

Dr. Zee: It's so funny. There are all these diagnoses for people who talk to themselves, like schizophrenia or dementia. But when you talk to yourself, and you say aloud things like, "I am beautiful. I am great," or when you look in the mirror and say, "I am wealthy. I am a queen,"—it actually gives your brain the momentum to say, "Oh my God, it's true." Why? Because you're feeling it. When you say, "I am ugly," the opposite is happening.

> First, when you say it, the world sees it because you're showing it. And second, when you say it, you believe it. You know that's you. You have to say it to yourself out loud. Looking in the mirror and saying this kind of thing out loud is the same as if someone else is telling you something negative. So, looking in the mirror and speaking your self-talk out loud is the best way to bring in more positivity and feelings of goodness.

To hear more of our interview, listen to Episode #31 of *The Breakdown with Bethany.*

Meet the Rule Breaker: Jennifer Lopez

I adore Jennifer Lopez. For many reasons, she is 100% my aspirational person, a person I'd love to meet and have on my show.

First, I've always been impressed with her journey. She'd be the first to tell you that she comes from the Bronx, Castle Hill Ave, and that her roots are in New York.

Second, she's so committed to the narrative of love. It's woven into her life and career. Love is the anchor and vessel for everything she does and creates. Talking about love causes us to reflect on our feelings of love and how we put love into the world, and it can make us feel vulnerable. But Jennifer Lopez's vulnerability is one reason why we love her so much. We've watched her make up, break up, and get back together over the last 20-plus years, yet she says she's just getting started.

I was surprised to learn from a 2018 article in *Harper's Bazaar* that she practices affirmations daily. She has pillows and signs with affirmations all over her home. I've tried to emulate Jennifer Lopez in many ways—from my hairstyle, clothing, and makeup to the way I talk and dance, but it wasn't until I read that article that I started copying the way that she thinks and acts.

Here's what Jennifer had to say to *Harper's Bazaar*[2] about using daily affirmations to fill her life with joy, gratefulness, and positivity.

"My life is full of loving and joyful people, and my workplace is filled with adventure," she says, quoting one of her favorite affirmations.

[Lopez], who repeats mantras like this to herself throughout the day, swears by the power of positive thinking.

"Affirmations are so important," she says earnestly. "I am youthful and timeless. I tell myself that every day, a few times a day. It sounds like clichéd bullshit, but it's not: Age is all in your mind. Look at Jane Fonda."

"When I was younger I spent a lot of time being half happy and half not happy," she says. The difference now? "I know who I am and what I want. I also know my strengths and weaknesses. It took me a long time to get to a point where I could say something nice about myself. I'm glad I can do that now."

Tips to Implement Right Now

1. Try talking to yourself positively in the mirror every day.
2. Practice positive self-talk by saying things like:
    - "You got this, baby girl."
    - "More love, less fear."
    - "I am enough."
    - "I am in the right place, at the right time, doing the right thing."

- "I am capable of doing absolutely everything I dream of."
- "I am the hero in my life story."

3. Imagine encouraging your best friend at her lowest moment. What would you say? Now, say that to yourself!

Recognize	Reframe	Reconnect
Take notice when you're not only thinking negative self-talk- you're also saying it out loud. I'm guilty of this at times, and my kids have caught me and helped pull me out of it.	Would you talk to your five-year-old self like that? Think of the way you talk to your best friends and how you shower them with positivity.	Talk to yourself like you are your own best friend-make it a habit. Treat yourself with love by maintaining a loving mindset. Practice loving self-talk.

Bethany's Chapter Breakdown

It's not enough to treat yourself like your own best friend-you have to talk to yourself that way, too.

CHAPTER 3:

Bet on Yourself

"I don't like to gamble, but if there's one thing I'm willing to bet on, it's myself."

-Beyonce Knowles

Old Rule: Wait for the right opportunities to present themself to create an amazing life.
New Rule: Create your own opportunities and remember that you are limitless.

As a 17-year-old freshman at New York University (NYU), I was going through a lot of things. I had just been diagnosed with diabetes, so I was stuck at home managing a disease and the angst that came with it at a time when I was supposed to be leaving home and striking out on my own. Instead, I was thrust back into my parent's arms. Craving independence as I was made it a difficult time.

So, during that first semester at NYU, I was just going through the motions. I wasn't present; I was checked out, angry, and anxious. At the end of the first semester, I got an evaluation from an amazing teacher that has stuck with me to this day, 20 years later: "Bethany does what is asked of her without asking anything of herself."

What? It took me a minute to understand what she meant. It was so against how I felt about myself: Determined, outspoken, sassy. That teacher—a voice instructor in my acting program at NYU—told me I'd never forget her. I guess she was right. The words on that evaluation are branded in my memory; I've turned them into a sort of mantra: "What do I ask of myself?" At work, in love, and in motherhood, I find myself reflecting on those words in a way that forces me to be accountable—to myself. [Sidebar: I recently looked that teacher up and saw that she's now one of the leading circus directors in the nation. She's directed the Big Apple Circus and is one of the main clowns. Talk about betting on yourself.]

About 10 years after I received that evaluation, I landed on a career choice. I wanted to be a writer.

There was just one problem—I didn't have any experience as a writer. My only "work" experience was waiting tables, bartending, crappy retail jobs, and getting pregnant. But I knew I could be a writer, and when I had my first opportunity, I gathered up all my self-doubt, chucked it out the window, and doubled down on my ambition, hoping that whoever interviewed me would see my drive and eagerness to learn. I bet on myself, and I hoped my future boss would, too.

She did—she hired me based on my personality, drive, and experience with motherhood, even though I had zero experience as a writer. This boss also hired me again a few years later…women are incredible and have so much unified power when they wield it for good.

It only takes one person to believe in you and give you a chance. My former boss did that for me. She saw something in me, gave me an opportunity, and became a great cheerleader for me. I was a new mom to a nine-month-old baby, and I was starting my first real job, but I trusted that everything would fall into place. Sometimes you need to take a risk. This was a big one, but I knew that I could learn and learn fast.

Six years after that first job, I started a new practice: Envisioning things and speaking them to myself to make them a reality. Today, I'm a testament to this practice in many ways, but mostly with regard to my career. I have blended my vision of my professional journey with feelings of gratitude and created a career that I'm proud of and leaves me in a bit of disbelief. I'm an editor, a writer, and an author. I've also appeared on television—a dream I developed in the midst of my editing career. These things might not seem like a big deal, but I wished for and visualized every one of these accomplishments.

Watching your dreams unfold in real-time is somewhat surreal, but I'm doing it through the

power of positive thinking and my strong belief in myself. Of course, there have been many setbacks, rejections, and embarrassing failures along the way. But each time I flopped, I came back to what I knew about myself—my work ethic, my ability to learn, and my desire to succeed—and I felt confident and unafraid to go after the next item on the agenda. So, I'd take the next step, apply for the next job, or go after something I wasn't quite qualified for because I believed in myself.

When I was younger, the idea of creating my own opportunities was overwhelming, so much so that I would sometimes shut down at the thought of it. I remember my parents telling me during my first internship, "Make yourself indispensable." But what does that mean? Does it mean doing the job of 20 people? Does it mean coming up with a new filing system for the company? The whole notion was vague and confusing to me.

It wasn't until I had my kids and experience with working and struggling and coming up against challenges that I realized that creating your own opportunities means following your passions and putting some energy behind it.

When I was working for big publishing companies, I sometimes met with pushback, and I sometimes met with appreciation. But outside validation or rejection isn't important. What's important is to continue to take actionable steps toward the life you want, personally or professionally.

When I had my children, I wasn't married. But I knew I wanted to be a mother, so I created an opportunity for myself to become the best mom I could possibly be, despite the

less-than-perfect circumstances of my life. When I decided to pursue a career in journalism, I had no educational background in journalism. I hustled from the bottom of the ladder, first as an intern, then as an assistant, then as associate editor, senior editor, and ultimately overseeing a publication. There were times when I didn't feel like betting on myself, when I felt overwhelmed, unqualified, or like an imposter—despite having the support of my parents and friends. The only person who *has* to bet on you is *you*.

In her book *Lean In*, Sheryl Sandberg—former chief operating officer at Facebook—wrote that women will only apply to a job if they meet 100% of the qualifications, while men will apply if they meet 60% of the qualifications.[1] In a 2010 TED Talk,[2] she said:

> Women systematically underestimate their own abilities. If you test men and women, and you ask them questions on totally objective criteria like GPAs, men get it wrong slightly high, and women get it wrong slightly low. Women do not negotiate for themselves in the workforce. A study in the last two years of people entering the workforce out of college showed that 57% of [men] are negotiating their first salary—and only 7% of women [do the same]. And most importantly, men attribute their success to themselves, and women attribute it to other external factors. If you ask men why they did a good job, they'll say, "I'm awesome." . . . If you ask women why they did a good job, what they'll say is, someone helped them, they got lucky, they worked really hard. Why does this matter? Boy, it matters a lot. Because no one gets to the corner office by sitting on the side, not at the table. And no one gets the promotion if they don't think they deserve their success.

Spotlight: Laura Casselman

Laura Casselman moved from small-town America to New York City to pursue simultaneous careers in the corporate world and professional dancing. This inspiring woman has led numerous companies to success as VP of Operations, COO, and CEO. Her new book *Trust Your Increments* shows "How small, consistent steps can lead to massive success."

I thought her interview would be perfect for this chapter. Here's what Laura had to say in our interview about changing the rules for women in the workplace.

Bethany: Tell me a little bit about your background.

Laura: I grew up in a one-stoplight town where we had three television channels. I lived in my imagination if you can wrap your head around that. I just wanted to get out and see the world. But on one of our three channels, I got to see the Macy's Thanksgiving Day parade, and I saw the Rockettes and all their glam and the kick line, and I was like, "I'm going to do that." From the time I was three years old when I declared I was going to be a Rockette, until after college, when I finally went to New York and auditioned, that was my life plan. I was going to be a Radio City Rockette. And I did, and it was wonderful. I got to fulfill my childhood dreams.

People always say, "Oh, New York City can chew you up and spit you out." But I just say New York City made me grow up. It made me grow up. It made me see the world far differently than I ever saw it. I realized my childhood dreams, and then I transitioned into corporate America. When I retired from dancing, I stepped into my first executive position because I had done dual resume the entire time. And then realized, wow, this is not exactly what I thought it would be. And so, here I am now, leading companies and saying, "When you get to the place where you can change the rules, it is our responsibility to change the rules."

Bethany: Tell me, actually—because I wasn't planning on asking this—but tell me about some of the rules you broke or changed to get to where you are now.

Laura: Well, one of the things I did is that I did play by the rules a lot. I played by the rules because I felt, at first, like I didn't have to, and then I got penalized. I was consistently penalized for not playing by the rules or for speaking up too often. I was becoming difficult to work with, and that happens to women a lot. I said, "Let me play by the rules. I will beat you at your own game." And that is what I became stoked to do. "I will play by your rules, and I will still win."

And winning wasn't proving them wrong. Winning was accomplishing my own goals. I had a shift in my thinking: This isn't about you; it's about me. And the moment I did that, and the moment I said, "I get it. You've made it clear. I accept these rules, and I also know I am capable." That's how I got to where I am now, where I can change the rules. I don't want other women fighting the same fight I fought, and I certainly don't want my daughter to do it when she has the choices in her life of what she wants to do or become.

Bethany: Something that we've heard about—seen firsthand, probably even experienced firsthand as women, as mothers in the workplace—is the dramatic or traumatic leaving of the workplace that women had to do in the last two years. I want to know your thoughts about that and about where women are at now. I've heard a lot about a reemergence or career shifts, and I would love to know from your side of things what that looks like.

Laura: I think prior to the pandemic, we were having a discussion: "Hey, women have all these other responsibilities aside from their jobs. We take care of the majority of household requirements. We take care of our older parents. We take care of our children, and school requirements. There are a lot of requirements on our plate in addition to what we see for males—they generally go to work, come home, get to play with the kids, have more fun, more freedom. They're not the people saying, 'We've got to do this, we've got to do that. Your homework must be done, dinner's got to be cooked.'"

And it was hard, I think, for people to wrap their minds necessarily around it because they were like, "No, it's 2019. There's not this much inequality." And then the pandemic hit, and I think people realized, "Hey, we can't do this. I can't work at home unless someone is handling the kid. Someone's got to clean up, someone's still got to cook dinner."

And people started to realize that women are the ones doing it. And we saw so many women leave the workforce in order to do it and homeschool their kids. So, when we see this massive step back, we realize we were already over 200 years out from equal pay, and now we've stepped even further back, which is painful to look at now.

I think we have to realize that there has been a mind shift in the younger generation. They're saying, "We don't want to break through that glass ceiling anymore. This is ridiculous. We are just beating our heads." I saw an article recently that said, "We want to walk out of the building. We want to leave the building completely."

But I just had a conversation with someone who kind of enlightened me, and gave me a new way to look at it: "There is no glass ceiling. There is no building. We just are. What are we going to do?"

And I thought, what a great way to put it. We just are. What are we going to do with our lives, with our choices? And I know for me—my choices—I'm going to make sure that things are better when I'm done.

To hear more of our interview, listen to Episode #20 of *The Breakdown with Bethany.*

Meet the Rule Breaker: Keke Palmer

Keke Palmer is an actress and singer who's performed on Broadway and in hit movies. Although she began her acting career in 2003, it wasn't until a couple of years ago that she showed up on my radar. I'm in awe of this talented, multifaceted human being. I haven't met her personally, but she seems to be herself at every turn. She embodies confidence and kindness, and she is so freaking funny.

Here's what Keke has to say in her book, *I Don't Belong to You*,[3] on belonging to herself.

> The choices we make determine the experiences we have. We can decide to just drift along and let the voices in our head control us, or we can remain conscious and be a force in directing where we want our lives to go. I learned that my destiny belonged to me and that the present moment belonged to me. I belonged to me, and I had to have my back and I had to have enough awareness to make the right choices for me. That's the first step. In life, before we can make a good conscious decision about what we're going to eat for dinner, what activities we're going to do, what job suits us best, who we want to date, and what we're going to do—pretty much any choice we're going to make at all—we have to first determine who we belong to by accepting that we are responsible for ourselves. And we can be guided by whatever it is in our lives that stirs our passion and inspires us to dream.

Tips to Implement Right Now

In life, it's easy to get caught up in the mundane and forget what we're working toward—or maybe even realize that we are not working toward anything we are passionate about. Our passions can fall by the wayside, and our goals can become nothing more than daydreams. But what if we could channel our energy into something tangible, something that moves us closer to our goals?

Here are a few ways to move toward your purpose every day:

1. Make a list of your talents and your passions. Give yourself permission to dream big!
2. Be ready to deliver—preparation is key to delivering on the promise that you are the real deal. Do your research and be ready to go when an opportunity arises. Maybe it's applying for a job or figuring out how to raise money from investors. Knowledge is power.
3. Speak the dream into existence. Bet on yourself and know that your dream is possible.
4. Get training. I had a dream to be on TV, so I hired a coach to help me show up on camera. I took classes and talked to on-air personalities and producers to get tips. These steps were huge catalysts in helping me achieve my dream.

Recognize	**Reframe**	**Reconnect**
Recognize when you're not betting on yourself-when you're holding yourself back in relationships, work, or your personal growth because you don't feel qualified.	Think about what the process of moving toward your goal will look like. Use affirmations to validate your worthiness, move forward, and bet on yourself.	Reconnect with your purpose. Seek additional resources to help you get to where you want to go. Invest in yourself by taking a class or submitting a job application.

Bethany's Chapter Breakdown

You never lose when you bet on yourself.

Part 2:
Friends, Lovers, and Others

"If you can't love yourself, how in the hell are you going to love somebody else?"
-RuPaul

Now that we've discussed ways to love yourself and put yourself first, let's talk about how we bring that love to our relationships.

This is tricky, even for me. I have many relationships that I would define as codependent— that's something I'm still working on. But choosing myself first allows me to bring my best to a relationship, even if it's a work in progress.

A relationship is a place we go to *give*, not receive. The things we need to receive—like love, worth, and validation—have to come from within. We can't expect anyone to give us those things, and that expectation is likely why most relationships fail. If we give ourselves what we need to in order to thrive, we can go into our relationships with a giving mindset without feeling like we're losing out.

In the following three chapters, we'll dive into navigating tricky relationships, setting healthy boundaries, and making sure we give ourselves what we want to receive from others.

CHAPTER 4:

I Now Denounce You

"Love is a vessel that contains both security and adventure, and commitment offers one of the great luxuries of life: time. Marriage is not the end of romance, it is the beginning."

-Esther Perel

Old Rule: Give all of yourself to have a successful relationship.
New Rule: Continue to put yourself first, even in relationships.

Relationships can be so tricky. When we're young, we're taught that we should have a goal of having a steady partner—marriage, a wedding, kids, the white picket fence, growing old together, happily ever after. Yada yada yada. But no one prepares us for the nitty-gritty of the day-to-day experience of being with someone. Of falling in love with someone, you have nothing in common with. Of the little fights that can escalate into big ones.

This is what we need to be prepared for. We don't need images of elaborate weddings or picture-perfect depictions of motherhood. Sharing your life with someone is hard, and I think we often approach relationships the wrong way.

One of the preconceived notions we have about relationships is that we need to give ourselves up, compromise, or sacrifice to be in a relationship. But that's not true at all. In fact, the opposite is true.

My relationship with my husband is atypical. We met as teens and dated casually. Then dated seriously. Broke up. Got back together. Broke up again. Got back together again. Had two kids. Then we got married. Twenty years later, it still feels like we're on a journey of growth, acceptance, and love.

It's hard for me to go into details about my relationship with my husband. There's certainly much to unpack. But one critical point is that you have to have trust. Without trust, you don't have a foundation to build on.

And, of course, you have to trust your partner—but you also have to trust yourself. I decided to get pregnant and have kids before I got married. I did it because I wanted that for myself. I wanted to be a mother. I didn't give much thought to anything else—my career or my relationship with my boyfriend (now my husband). I planned on figuring it all out later—and let me tell you, I'm still working on that. It's a work in progress, something I'm continuing to figure out. But I held strong to my belief that what I was doing was right because it was what I wanted. Becoming a mother was all I could think about. I decided to bet on myself, knowing that regardless of the circumstances of my relationship with their father, my kids would have a foundation of love, and has proved itself to be very true.

But there were periods of time when I felt like I was living in sin and doing my kids a disservice because I didn't marry their father. It took me a few years to realize that my desire to have children, the love I gave my children, and the life I created so they could feel safe and secure was enough. Any decisions I made that veered from that desire and love were due to outside pressure, my own feelings of insecurity, or a desire to live up to others' expectations. Choices made on that kind of basis always come back to bite you in the ass.

What do you do if you're in a relationship that isn't working, whether it's a romantic relationship, a friendship, or a parent–child relationship? There's a good chance it's not working because you've given away too much of yourself because you're living according to someone else's expectations rather than aligning with what's going on within you.

There's a weird dichotomy between men and women (more than one). A recent TikTok trend illustrates it—videos that show women saying how stressed and anxious they are and then pan to their husbands, who are clearly *not* stressed and are dancing around in their underwear (or doing something equally ridiculous). I asked my husband if he wanted to say anything about our relationship for this chapter. Something about how we're still together, working through our shit, after 20 years and two kids. About our insight into how two totally different people with different cultural backgrounds, values, and opinions can cohabitate with joy. He replied, "No, but I would like a snack." Fucking men!

We build the most meaningful and fulfilling relationships when we put ourselves first. If we put ourselves first, we never feel like we're giving too much away in our relationships. This has certainly been my case. It's a constant balancing act, back and forth. We're encouraged to choose our spouse, and we do choose them over and over again, walking through the good and the bad, for better or worse. But we also have to choose ourselves over and over again, too. These two choices aren't mutually exclusive: they're mutually *inclusive*. If we choose ourselves, if we give ourselves the love we give others, our relationships have a better chance of thriving. There's less room for resentment, which makes more room for— you guessed it—love.

My husband and I met when we were 18-year-old kids before we were fully formed adults. Our individual growth and maturing had to take place within the framework of our relationship. It's hard enough to grow on your own; growing in the context of a relationship was even more challenging. But I love my husband, and I've chosen him over and over again. I think the reason why our relationship continues to be successful—and we can measure success by the fact that we're still together, that we have more happy moments than unhappy moments, and we're raising our family—is because I've never felt like our relationship contradicted what I wanted. I've never felt compelled to compromise my own thoughts and opinions or my desires for my life. I've been able to come back to myself again and again. You *can* choose yourself over and over again and still have a successful romantic relationship, whatever that looks like for you.

This chapter is titled "I Now Denounce You." I chose that title because I felt a lot of shame about being an unwed mother. Women often feel shame, whether they're in relationships or single. People don't talk about things they think are shameful. Divorce is a good example. I was talking to someone who was recently divorced and had started dating. She told me, "I don't want my date to know that I've been divorced twice." But you know what? Life happens. We need to be okay with that.

It doesn't matter what someone else thinks or says; what matters is what we think or say about ourselves. We allow other people to judge us, and that's not right. Many times we're judged not by another person but by *ourselves.* Our self-talk is about our feelings of shame: "No one in my family has been divorced. Now I'm divorced, and it's a shame." Or, "No one in my family has ever been an ambitious career woman who has to travel and leave their kids at home with a nanny. That's a shame." We tell ourselves these things.

We can use the 3Rs to adjust our thinking. First, you need to recognize the feeling of shame. You might think it's coming from someone else, but it's most likely coming from you. Once you recognize the shame, you have to reframe it. Gabby Bernstein says when you're feeling stuck, anxious, hurt, lost—or, in this case, shameful—you can pick the next-best thought or feeling for yourself. She calls this the "Choose Again Method,"[1] and I have used it many, many times. For example, shame is a heavy emotion. You can take a small step toward reframing shame by thinking of the next-best emotion or thought. When I'm feeling ashamed about having been an unwed mother, I can take the power away from the shame like this: I start out thinking, "I'm the only mother in the world who's not married. There's nobody else like me." But I know I'm not alone; I'm not the only unmarried mom. That's how I reframe the sense of shame. I reframe my thought to, "I'm not the only one."

Another way I've dealt with shame is to do some physical things that ground me. I might start by noticing my surroundings. What do I smell? What do I see? What do I feel? What do I hear? I also might change my surroundings by going outside or doing something to get my mind off the sense of shame to separate myself from it. This helps me reconnect with myself and takes away the power of shame.

Spotlight: Arica Angelo

Arica Angelo is a top relationship coach and the host of Bravo's *Love Without Borders*. I knew I wanted to include a conversation with a relationship expert in this book, but I wasn't expecting to be able to talk to one of the best in the biz! In our interview, Arica dropped some serious knowledge about *interdependency*—a word I had never heard before—and how we can continue to give energy to our long-term relationships.

Here's what she had to say about the importance of interdependence and how to keep your relationships healthy.

Bethany: I'll give you a little bit of my background. My husband and I have been dating since we were 18. Now, we're hitting our 20-year mark this year, believe it or not. It's been kind of wild—two kids, the death of a parent—the things life throws at us. How do you prioritize a relationship, keep a relationship healthy, in moments when you've torn away from it or don't feel like giving energy to the relationship—and yet the relationship is so important to you?

Arica: That's a question we don't ask ourselves enough. And I'll include myself in that. I've never experienced the loss of a parent, and I'm not looking forward to that day. So, I'm sorry that you guys went through that on top of having a life and a marriage and children—that's a lot of responsibility. It's a lot to carry.

So, in these changes of life—as you go through things, and you're pulled in different directions— check in with your heart. Have a conversation with your heart. I think of my heart as a person, an infinite being that lives inside of me and has all the wisdom, all the answers. If I don't check in with my, I'll never get access to any of that wisdom. I need to groom that relationship, check in with my heart, and say, "You've been through a lot. What do you need right now?"

Sometimes when you've been giving and giving, your heart's like, "I don't have the capacity to give anything to myself, but this is what I could use from other people." And that's beautiful in itself. That's a healthy neediness, an interdependence. Have the courage to allow your heart to have a voice and speak about what your heart needs to others. It might be something as silly as telling your partner, "I could really use a foot massage."

When you check in with yourself, you can ask, "Do I need something physical? Do I need something verbal? Do I need time alone?" That cultivates your relationship with your heart. For those who come from a biblical background, the Bible says, "The heart is the wellspring of life." The heart is our wellspring. It's living within us. We can blend our relationship with our heart into our conversations with our partner and be like, "Hey, I've never said this to you, but how am I showing up for your heart? What does your heart need from me? What can I give you?" Often, these are the conversations that we don't want to have, because they can go so many different directions. No matter what direction they go in, it's like putting on a pair of ice skates and sliding around, navigating things together.

Maybe your partner says, "I need more sex." And you're exhausted. You've been wiping children's butts all day, and you don't feel very sexy. Okay, great—have that conversation: "I'm not feeling very sexy right now. I have no energy." I don't want to get explicit, but you might discuss how to help you get in the mood—maybe bring in some extra help, like a toy. I'm not trying to be vulgar; what I'm saying is, *have* that messy conversation. Check in with your heart first, and then talk to your partner.

When the demands are too great, get out on the ice rink and slip around. Talk until you find common ground. Is that making any sense?

Bethany: My next question I wasn't planning on asking, but you said the word *interdependence.* I've never heard that word before. I've heard *codependent,* and I know something about that. But interdependence sounds really interesting—like something I want to achieve. Tell us about interdependence and how it's vital to healthy relationships.

Arica: Oh, heck yes. A girlfriend told me about this concept; it was something her father taught her. I'm stealing it from her—shout out to my girlfriend Jesse. We are taught self-love and independence, especially in Western cultures, but that's all rubbish. It's garbage. There's an element of truth to it, but *just* an element. It's not the full picture.

We know the concept that it takes a village to raise a child. When you came into the world, you weren't a lone ranger. You needed mom and dad to hook up. You needed mom's belly to hold you and her lower region to birth you. Then you needed a team of doctors to pull you out. You didn't come into the world alone. So what on earth makes you think that you're supposed to be a lone ranger, doing it all on your own? That's complete nonsense—too much independence. We need each other.

I can fill my own cup, but if in my relationship there are things that I need from my partner, guess what? That's okay. That doesn't make me needy or insecure. If you don't know how to fill your cup, then we need to talk about that. But needing another human being is one of the most beautiful things we get to share with one another. I hear singles say, "I'm good on my own. I just want someone to be the cherry on top of the cake. I just want them to be the icing." And I'm like, "No, they're not the icing.

> They're the butter and eggs. They go into your cake. We need each other." It's beautiful.
>
> That's what I mean by interdependence. We came into the world needing someone. And if you someone, especially a single person, "What's your biggest fear?" they're likely to say, "I don't want to end up alone." Why are we so afraid of being alone? We legitimately *should* be afraid of being alone because that's not how it's supposed to be. We're not *supposed* to be alone. We're supposed to *need* each other. It's okay and it's beautiful to need each other.

To hear more of our interview, listen to Episode #35 of *The Breakdown with Bethany.*

Meet the Rule Breaker: Tara Schuster

Tara Schuster is like the girlfriend that you don't know personally but who is always there with supportive advice. In this case, it's in the form of a book that you can refer back to time and time again.

I discovered Tara through her first book, *Buy Yourself the F*cking Lilies.* The title drew me in, and after reading the first few pages, I knew she was someone I needed in my life. Although I don't know her personally, Tara's words have helped me immensely.

Here's an excerpt from *Buy Yourself the F*cking Lilies*[2] on how the relationship with yourself is your most important one. I think it resonates with this chapter.

> To calm myself, I brought to mind the love I knew I had: my own. I had been working on taking care of

myself for so long that I now had an arsenal of tools to give myself love. I once heard the magnificent, enlightened Elizabeth Gilbert say that "true love liberates the beloved. You are your beloved. You liberate yourself." Those words called out to me like a benevolent siren song, impossible to ignore. (And as you can guess, they now live on my Idea Board—held up with gold glitter tape, obvi.) Instead of choosing a moment with my family, I looked for the times I had soothed and loved and liberated myself. I recalled a particularly warm and decadent bath I had recently drawn after a boy had broken up with me. I remembered playing with the warm suds around me and saying aloud, "I am good." I thought of a solo hike I had taken on a trail in Malibu. I had gone farther than I thought I was capable of. I felt the orange sun wash over me as I leaped between boulders, exhilarated and free and a little scared but totally at peace with myself. I could see the lilies I bought regularly simply because I believed I was worth lilies. Unconditional love started with me deciding that no matter whether I was successful, no matter what other people thought of me, I would always believe in myself. I was my beloved.

Tips to Implement Right Now

1. Ask your partner for what you want or need. Maybe it's space. Maybe it's more quality time together. But you won't get it if you don't ask.
2. If you're going to ask for something, be ready to give. Listen to your partner with an open heart and mind.

3. Practice vulnerability. I know it's hard—it is for me, too. Take it slowly. Try sharing things like fears and insecurities the moment they bubble up.

Recognize	Reframe	Reconnect
Learn to recognize when you're giving away too much in a relationship. A good indicator is feeling lonely when your partner is right next to you. That's a signal that you're out of alignment. We're taught that the best relationships are selfless ones, but selfless relationships don't feel good.	If you feel lost or lonely in your relationship, take that as a sign that it's time to start reconnecting to yourself. It might feel sad or scary, but signs like these are important, and they shouldn't be looked at negatively. Imagine if you never noticed and continued on feeling unfulfilled. No thanks!	Start reconnecting to yourself and your self-love practice. Repeat positive affirmations in the mirror or go sign up for a dance class. Do something for you that's fun and completely selfish. Start filling your own cup and watch how it changes the dynamics in your relationships.

Bethany's Chapter Breakdown

To have a better connection with your partner, keep connecting to yourself.

CHAPTER 5:

Boundaries Can Be a Real Bitch

"Daring to set boundaries is about having the courage to love ourselves, even when we risk disappointing others."

-Brene Brown

Old Rule: You don't need to set boundaries with the people you're closest to.
New Rule: The most successful relationships have boundaries. It's often with the people we love the most that boundaries are required.

Boundaries are a popular topic right now. Everyone from Jada Pinkett Smith to Mel Robbins is talking about how to set and maintain boundaries. I guess I'm throwing another log on the fire.

Although boundaries are a hot topic, we don't often take the time to figure out what boundaries we need and implement them.

If we do implement boundaries, we don't often *stick* to them. Why? Because it's freaking hard.

As mothers, we're prone to give, give, give. Even "selfish" or "spoiled" moms often feel like they give until there's nothing left. How do we set boundaries with our small children? With our mothers, who've given us everything? With our partners, who love us unconditionally? I'm working on this myself, but here's what I figured out so far: Boundaries aren't there to keep people *away*; boundaries are there to keep you sane and whole so that you can have *closer* relationships.

I feel drained at times by my kids, my mom, and my husband, and setting boundaries with them is extremely challenging. Sometimes they take so much from me without giving anything back. Instead of resenting them, I set boundaries. Not even marriage is a

boundary-free relationship. The boundaries I set allow me to come back to loving myself first and filling my own cup. At first glance, it might seem rude or disconnected to set boundaries for people you love. But you're setting those boundaries so you can come back to them with more love, energy, and willingness to participate in the relationship.

The thought of setting boundaries may stress you out, but they're necessary in all our relationships: with spouses, kids, parents, colleagues, neighbors, and friends. Boundaries are limits we set on ourselves and others to protect ourselves emotionally and physically. They help us feel safe and secure and prevent others from taking advantage of us.

It's difficult to establish and maintain boundaries. However, it's important to do so in order to protect your time, energy, and sanity. You can use self-talk to gain clarity on what you need. Then, communicate your needs without feeling guilty, and don't be afraid to say no.

Recently, I realized that the sense of betrayal and the general yuckiness I felt when

someone crossed a boundary isn't something I should blame myself for. I also realized that I can do something about those feelings. It might sound silly, but sometimes we need permission to feel empowered. When you feel the betrayal and malaise that comes with violated boundaries, give yourself that permission.

Here's an example. I used to let people dominate conversations, even if what they were saying was offensive to me. I used to be afraid of sharing opinions (still working on that). Most of all, I used to be afraid of confrontation. But over time—mostly by watching powerful women take up space—I realized that I deserve to take up space, too. Adjectives that used to define me—nonconfrontational, objective, impartial, nonchalant—were defense mechanisms. I maintained those characteristics so I wouldn't need to feel dissatisfied with people crossing my boundaries. But I empowered myself by emulating powerful women. I decided to stop playing small. Sure, I'm still objective; I'm still a good listener. But I know how to set boundaries, and I know how to walk away when they're crossed time and time again.

Spotlight: Ericka Day

Ericka Day is a burnout, corporate transitions, and boundary coach. Her work is heavily influenced by Terri Cole, who was a teacher of mine at NYU.

She joined me on my podcast to talk about setting and resetting boundaries and how important they are for our self-care.

Bethany: What are some actionable steps that women can take to fight against how they've been conditioned?

Ericka: Well, I think the first step is always knowledge. Knowledge is power. When you come up against a pattern that is ingrained in our society, you should realize that you're not alone because suffering persists in silence. The next step is to actually start to shift your perspective.

View the boundaries you want to create in your life as nourishment for you, your deepest values, and your energy. So often, we're so worried about letting others down, but the reality is that if we don't set boundaries and begin to step into our lives, we let *ourselves* down. And that has a ripple effect on our lives—if we aren't able to set boundaries, we feel resentful and unhappy. We suffer from mental fatigue; we feel exhausted and depleted. When that happens, we're not going to be able to show up as the powerful women that we are.

Bethany: Boundaries are something we're hearing a lot about lately. It's kind of a buzzword. What I'm specifically interested in is this: I've heard that the boundaries we most need are usually with the people we're closest to. How do you help women—especially mothers—understand when to set boundaries with their kids or parents or spouses?

Ericka: I like to do what I call a boundary audit. For example, if you're a mother, you look at your relationships and start asking yourself, "What's working for me? What isn't working?" If you have patterns of resentment building in an area of your life, that's a sign that a boundary needs to be set. Perhaps you feel like you're doing most of the emotional labor at home. Dive into that. Ask yourself what is and what isn't working in that area. You might write some things down, and you might need to communicate with your partner. As women, we sometimes hold resentment but don't have the conversation with our partner. Maybe we haven't given them the chance to change their behavior.

Start with a boundary audit. Then, communicate from a place of love. And there's a process that's helpful for this, especially if this is your first time setting a boundary with someone—it can be scary. First, just state the issue. Second, state your feelings about the issue. Third, make a simple request. And last, maybe suggest an agreement.

An example of this could be, maybe your sister is constantly borrowing your clothing without asking you, and then you get upset with her. So, you might say, "Hey Valerie, I've noticed that you've been borrowing my clothes without asking, and this is causing me feelings of resentment because some of these pieces I really want to wear. I was wondering if, in the

> future if you want to borrow my clothes, would you be willing to ask me in advance?" That illustrates how you go through the process of setting a boundary.
>
> Setting boundaries with someone for the first time can be difficult. But you need to ask yourself, "Have I had a conversation with this person and gotten specific about what's bothering me?" If you tell your husband, "Oh my gosh, I'm so mad at you," but you don't know why, you need to do a boundary audit and ask yourself specifically what's going on.

To hear more of our interview, listen to Episode #37 of *The Breakdown with Bethany.*

Meet the Rule Breaker: Glennon Doyle

I have a hard time writing about the people who are most impactful in my life. Part of me wants to keep their impact sacred and personal. But since Glennon is so public not only as a person but also with her thoughts, struggles, fears, and emotions, it makes sense for me to tell you what she means to me.

I first discovered Glennon years ago when she was known as a "Christian Mommy Blogger." Her first book, *Carry On, Warrior,* rocked my soul, and her second book, *Love Warrior,* broke my heart. Her third book, *Untamed,* brought me back to life. I bought it as an audiobook, hardback, and e-book. You may have heard the phrase she coined, "We can do hard things"; it's now the name of her podcast. So it pretty much goes without saying that Glennon is my girl.

Glennon has a lot to say about boundaries, but I thought these quotes from *Untamed*[1] on knowing when your boundaries have been crossed were perfect for this chapter. She describes anger as a "delivery" that alerts her that a boundary has been crossed. Accepting the "delivery" leads to new information about herself.

> Anger delivers important information about where one of our boundaries has been crossed. When we answer the door and accept that delivery, we begin to know ourselves better.
>
> When we restore the boundary that was violated, we honor ourselves. When we know ourselves and honor ourselves, we live with integrity, peace, and power—understanding that we are the kind of woman who will be wise and brave enough to care for herself. . . .
>
> Even better stuff comes when we go deeper. When we say, "Okay. I understand that this is my boundary." But what is a boundary anyway? A boundary is the edge of one of our root beliefs about ourselves and the world.

Tips to Implement Right Now

1. Start with self-reflection. If you don't know what boundaries you need, you won't be able to set them.
2. Start with just a few boundaries—perhaps one or two—and commit to being consistent with them.
3. Take time to reflect. Are your boundaries working? Do you need to change them up? Do they need to be reset? Boundaries are an ever-evolving thing.

Recognize	Reframe	Reconnect
It's fairly easy to know when your boundaries have been crossed. For me, a feeling of betrayal comes up. I feel anxious and unsettled. Once you learn how you respond emotionally to someone crossing a boundary, you'll have an easier time recognizing when it happens.	When someone has crossed a boundary, try not to be reactive. Reframe the boundary crossing as a signal that something needs to be done. Instead of acting from a place of anger or hurt, remind yourself and the boundary crosser why the boundary was created in the first place. Take the situation as an opportunity to honor yourself once again.	Enforcing a boundary is a protection, so don't be afraid to remind someone who crossed a boundary why it was put there in the first place. Sometimes boundaries need to be reinforced. People that love you won't be offended by this. Boundaries are for everyone's protection. Reconnecting to your boundaries is never finished.

Bethany's Chapter Breakdown

Set boundaries, and don't be afraid to reset them if they're crossed.

CHAPTER 6:

Roots and Wings

"Good parents give their children roots and wings. Roots to know where home is, wings to fly away and exercise what's been taught them."

-Jonas Salk

Old Rule: We can find happiness when we honor our parents, partners, and friends.
New Rule: Honor yourself and own your individuality.

Sometime after the birth of my second child, I was riding the train home one day and it dawned on me that I had done everything out of order: Kids first, career second, and marriage . . . who knew? By that time, I had checked kids off the list—that is, I *had* kids and that wasn't something that weighed on me anymore. And let me be very clear, I *wanted* kids, badly. I gave up pursuing a career as an actress (don't cry for me, I hated it), moved home from Los Angeles, and kissed my freewheeling twenties goodbye to become a mother—and I did it with a big smile on my face.

Babies first.

Once I ticked that box, I moved on to developing my career. But in between, I faced my fair share of criticism—from my parents, friends, priests, co-workers, and even new acquaintances.

As an only child, I felt a lot of pressure to honor my parents' wishes. In fact, I felt so much pressure that I ended up doing the opposite of their desires. My mother labeled me willful early on. I realized at quite a young age that I don't like being told what to do. I like to live for myself, not for others, and I'm easily triggered when others place expectations on me.

Even though my mother knew I wanted to have children before getting hitched, the first question she asked me and Manny after I got pregnant in 2011 was, "So, when are you getting married?" We just stared at her like she was nuts because that wasn't something we had discussed or wanted. I was 26, pregnant, jobless, living with my parents, and happily scared out of my mind.

Although I wanted to be a mom more than anything, the reality of my situation gave me good reason to be scared. But I fell back on my old habits: As an only child, I was used to getting what I wanted and not caring what anyone else thought about it. So, after a few weeks of doubting what I was doing, I reminded myself that I was doing exactly what I wanted to do.

There was nothing to doubt.

Looking back, a lot of the shame I felt, I placed on myself. My mother knew and accepted my desire to have a baby. The shame I felt about not meeting expectations or being unwed, was just antiquated bullshit I let get in my head. Don't be afraid to break the rules—to go against expectations set by parents, spouses, or bosses—to create a life that you love. Choosing yourself first in spite of the rules opens up all kinds of possibilities.

Now that my kids are 11 and 7 (as I write this), I want the same things for them that my

mother instilled in me. I want to give my children wings to fly and roots to know that they can always come home. If you're rooted and grounded, it gives you more freedom because when you're rooted in love and family, you have a safe place to land. You can go out and try new things, make mistakes, get hurt, and come home to lick your wounds in a safe place.

That's what helped me grow.

And if you don't have family support, you can give yourself roots and wings by being grounded in the love you give yourself. The 3Rs—recognize, reframe, and reconnect—give you a way to ground yourself, to set down roots that enable you to go after a job, into a relationship, or take a trip.

I was blessed with a great family that rooted me in love and gave me a strong sense of self-love. That enabled me to take risks. However, there have been times when I lost that feeling of being grounded. How do we get that feeling back? I think a lot of it has to do with being able to recognize, reframe, and reconnect.

Spotlight: Jennifer Uy

Jennifer Uy is a former television producer and founder of Empower PR.

Jen and I hit it off in our first meeting. She's in public relations, and I'm a writer, and the relationship between PR and media is a special one. We mutually depend on each other to get our jobs done. But Jen is also a friend. She's one of the first people I told about my dream of being on television. She saw something in me and helped me get my first dozen or so television segments, guiding me every step of the way— thanks to her television-producer background.

Here are a few questions I asked her about family, community, career, and being your own boss.

Bethany: Can you talk a bit about your career journey and shift to PR?

Jen: Before I was a publicist, I was a news producer for nearly 20 years. News taught me how to hustle, how to have thick skin, and how to do everything in a timely manner. I loved knowing that I was helping deliver important (and fun!) information to people every day.

I was working the early morning shift as an executive news producer when I had my son, and I had mom guilt big-time! News was my first "baby," so I couldn't wait to get back to work. But then I would have to go to sleep before my son went to bed and get up at 2 a.m. when he was still asleep to head to the station. I felt like I missed many little moments that I could never get back. When I got pregnant with my second child, I knew something had to give.

Becoming a publicist allowed me to be present for my family while still doing what I love and following my passion for telling stories, just in a different way.

Bethany: What drives you, day to day?

Jen: Knowing that I am helping someone else shine. Sharing people's stories and showcasing their brands in the best way possible makes me so happy! Being an entrepreneur is tough. So, just like my family and friends have supported me through the years, I aim to be that same cheerleader for my clients.

Also, family is everything to me. I want to make not only myself proud, but my family as well.

Bethany: Why did you decide to name your company Empower PR?

Jen: The word *empower* encompasses so much to me—strength, resilience, showing up for yourself and others—and that's exactly what I want to do for my clients.

Bethany: I know your community is important to you. How do you show up for them, and what are some ways they've shown up for you?

Jen: The simple act of showing up and supporting is key. I love championing hard workers, do-gooders, and everyday heroes. When people see that, they show up for you as well.

Bethany: Has there ever been a time when you felt like you were breaking a rule, when you had to go with your gut even if it went against your family or an antiquated "rule" you were taught?

Jen: I grew up in a strict Filipino household. It was disrespectful to answer back, question anything, or look at my mom in the eye when being reprimanded. For anyone wondering where I got my thick skin from—it started at home!

My mom, aunties, and uncles were really big on pursuing jobs that made lots of money—lawyer, doctor, things like that. I can't stand the sight of blood, but I loved to talk! I knew journalism was for me. When I started talking back and questioning things, my mom didn't like it at first. But through my hard work, she saw my passion. It didn't hurt that my grandpa loved the idea of me being a journalist, too!

Bethany: You were the first person to put me on television, and we've maintained an amazing personal and professional relationship. How do you cultivate professional relationships with women?

Jen: First of all, I LOVE YOU! When we met in person, I immediately knew you were special!

So many of us have been through *so* much, especially during the pandemic. Life is too short to be a bitch! Being a genuinely kind human is important. I make it a priority to check in on others and make sure they know I appreciate them and am cheering them on.

Bethany: What example are you hoping to set for your kids? What's your legacy?

Jen: It has always been a goal of mine to be my own boss. I want to make myself proud, my family proud, and most of all show my kids they can make their dreams come true with hard work, persistence, and a strong support system.

I want my kids to see me hustle, get frustrated, fail, succeed, be sad, and juggle everything—but keep moving forward.

Meet the Rule Breaker: Meghan Markle

I love Meghan Markle. I know she may be controversial to some, but when I look at her I see a woman who fell in love and refused to settle for anything less than she deserved. It was a long, hard road to Santa Barbara, but the Meghan we're seeing now is a woman to admire. She took on the monarchy so that she, her husband, and their children can live a life free of racism and family drama. Talk about a rule-breaker!

I was blown away by the docuseries *Harry & Meghan* on Netflix. Thinking about what Meghan Markle had to go through to fall in love with and marry the man of her dreams—the racism, the betrayals she faced—it was enough to destroy anybody. I admire her strength, her ability to speak her truth and advocate for others even as she was passing through what were probably the darkest moments of her life.

I don't think Meghan set out to break any rules, turn the monarchy on its head, or become a tabloid mainstay, although she's often painted as a woman with horrible ulterior motives. It's clear to me that she's not like that at all. I think her case shows how far we still have to go when it comes to supporting women—especially women of color—in their life choices.

Here are some things Meghan has said about women's empowerment and finding happiness.

> At the first annual Royal Family Foundation forum in February 2018:[1] I hear a lot of people saying—when speaking about girls empowerment, finding and knowing their worth, and women's empowerment as well—you'll often hear people say, 'Well, you're helping women finding their voices.' And I fundamentally disagree with that, because women don't need to find a voice; they have a voice, they need to feel empowered to use it, and people need to be encouraged to listen.
>
> In an August 2022 profile in *The Cut*, commenting on adjusting to royal life and being viewed as a princess:[2] [Control over her Instagram was just one of the things (along with The Tig, her passport, and the freedom to open her own mail) she gave up "It was a big adjustment—a huge adjustment to go from that kind of autonomy to a different life," says Meghan.
>
> "It's important to be thoughtful about [being seen as a princess] because—even with the [March 2021] Oprah interview, I was conscious of the fact that there are little girls that I meet and they're just like, 'Oh my God, it's a real-life princess.'" But her ambitions for herself (and the little girls who look up to her) are more than to marry into a position. "I just look at all of them and think, *You have the power within you to create a life greater than any fairy tale you've ever read.* I don't mean that in terms of 'You could marry a prince one

day.' I mean you can find love. You can find happiness. You can be up against what could feel like the greatest obstacle and then you can find happiness again."

Tips to Implement Right Now

1. If something's not working, don't be afraid to change it. Rules are made to be broken, especially if they aren't serving you or your family.
2. Cultivate your village—family, friends, or coworkers. Start to build a network of people that you can rely on.
3. Have some self-compassion. Apologize to yourself for past "mistakes," and don't let those "mistakes" hold you back from an incredible future.

Recognize	Reframe	Reconnect
Notice when you're feeling isolated and alone. One indicator might be that you're avoiding social interactions. Or maybe you're being extra hard on yourself for small things.	Take that feeling of isolation as an opportunity to practice positive self-talk. Use the positive affirmations from Chapters 2 and 3. Talk to yourself in a positive way to start building momentum toward a better mindset.	Reach out to friends and family. Reconnect with people you love and who love you. At the same time, reconnect with yourself. Start doing something you're passionate about- reading, writing, exercising, even starting a business-there's nothing too big or too small.

Bethany's Chapter Breakdown

Although no one is coming to save you,
saving yourself could mean asking for help.

Part 3:
Work and Ambition

"I think every working mom probably feels the same thing. You go through big chunks of time where you're just thinking, 'This is impossible-oh, this is impossible.' And then you just keep going and keep going, and you sort of do the impossible."

-Tina Fey

Here we are in Part 3. This was my favorite part of the book to write, perhaps because this is where I am in my life right now. I've done a lot of the work on myself—although it's never really *done*. And I've done a lot of the work on relationships—although that's also never really done. Now, I'm ready to run full speed into the career of my dreams. Putting these chapters together was a lot of fun, and I learned a lot along the way.

In Part 3, we'll dive into how you can start advocating for yourself in the workplace and climb ambitiously toward your dreams. We'll also see how cultivating a community and enlisting mentors can be extremely beneficial, both professionally and personally.

CHAPTER 7:

Working Girl

"I'm not gonna spend the rest of my life working my ass off and getting nowhere just because I followed rules that I had nothing to do with setting up, okay?"

-Melanie Griffith as Tess McGill in *Working Girl*

Old Rule: Wait until you feel like you're qualified to go for the opportunities you want.
New Rule: Go for it and learn on the job. Do things in ways that work for you.

I got my first real job when I was 26, just a few months before I got pregnant with my first child. I was back in New York City, having left an old dream behind in Los Angeles. In Los Angeles, I had been taking a continuing education class in broadcast journalism, which sparked my passion for journalism and media work.

(I also met one of my first mentors— more on that in Chapter 9.) Now, I was ready to start down the path to a career in journalism and media. I didn't have many resources or contacts at the time, so I searched for open opportunities in the field on Craigslist.

After feverishly sending out bullshit resumes to anyone and everyone that I thought could help me advance in editing, writing, or journalism, I landed a job at a production company as an intern. I didn't even get paid a stipend, but it was my first experience in digital media.

I was a 26-year-old pregnant intern, but I was probably the happiest I had ever been because things were starting to align. I felt like I had a purpose professionally, and I felt like I had a purpose personally. Although the path ahead wasn't clear, I knew I was headed exactly where I wanted to go. I just needed to keep putting one foot in front of the other in what I deemed to be the right direction.

I interned there for several months before finding a paid internship at a media agency. That felt more legitimate because they actually sent me out on real stories. It was a British-based tabloid media agency—not celebrity tabloid content; it focused on things that were trending at the time, things you might see on the TLC network.

My work there led to some pretty wild experiences. One of my assignments was to go "dining with the freegans"—that's a fancy British way of saying, dumpster diving. I went out to Rockaway to cover a dumpster diving feast! That was early in my pregnancy, so it was extra challenging trying to keep nausea at bay. It was fascinating. I got to meet all these cool people and tell their stories through my own eyes for a huge company. I think the piece ended up running in the New York Post (although I wasn't credited).

Another time, I sat in on an operation for a little girl with a facial deformity and reported on the before and after.

Those are a couple of highlights from my time as a 26-year-old pregnant intern. It was

fantastic. Sometimes in life, things just start to fall in place—signs from the universe or God or whatever you believe in. I was in some extreme situations that, at one time, I probably would have turned up my nose at—but there I was, excited to not only experience those things but also write about them for a real publication.

As my pregnancy progressed, I wasn't able to keep up with the demands of working as a poorly paid intern at an amazing media agency. I'm also a type 1 diabetic, which created some risks for my pregnancy, and I had to take a break.

Although I felt empowered and passionate about my career choice, there were definitely hiccups along the way. The first and foremost hiccup was that I didn't have any education or experience in the field of journalism. I thought I could quickly fix that by getting my second master's at the City University of New York School of Journalism. I'd learn all about grammar, syntax, journalism best practices, and ethics, find mentors, and then everything would fall into place. I'd leave my graduate program with an amazing job in my hometown and soar onward.

But of course, things never go as planned. I worked hard on my application, took admissions tests, interviewed, and took classes to help things along—I did all that only to be waitlisted. At that point, I was six or seven months into a high-risk pregnancy. I just wanted the damn job or an acceptance letter already. Instead, I paused my work at the media agency and my dream of a graduate degree in journalism to have my son.

Once Elias, my first son, arrived, my purpose was clearer. I wanted to be a journalist, and I wanted my work as a journalist to inform my personal life and vice versa. I like to say that I birthed my child and the idea for my career at the same time. Elias was my inspiration to get into parenting journalism because I figured that if I was a good writer and a good enough mom, then I could be a good parenting journalist.

Once again, I searched Craigslist and found a job as a New York City mommy blogger (for a website that no longer exists). It was my first experience doing what I really wanted to do. I took my new baby all around the city, experienced amazing things, wrote about them—and then got paid. One thing led to another; I found new opportunities in parenting journalism or related niches and climbed the ladder, eventually landing my dream job at a dream company.

It's a funny thing, to find your passion just as you jump head-on into motherhood. Many women wait until they are settled in their careers before thinking about motherhood. Other women prioritize children and then enter or reenter the workforce. Not many have kids and start their careers at the same time. But that's exactly what I did. In fact, if I hadn't become a mother when I did, I most likely would not have had the jobs I did.

As many women know, the path to a dream job is never easy, especially when we're raising kids in the process. My situation was atypical—I was a young mom but an old employee. I wasn't old by traditional standards; I was in my late twenties. But it felt old to start an

entry-level position with no relevant education to prop me up. There were times when I was embarrassed about my age and skills (or lack thereof), but I knew I was doing what I wanted to do, so I kept pushing forward.

When it comes to climbing the career ladder, you have to just go for it. Don't let your apparent lack of qualifications hold you back because *everyone* is trying to figure it out as they go along. You have to advocate for yourself in the workplace—as a woman and especially as a mother. I busted my butt as a new mom. I felt inadequate both at work and at home, but I kept pushing because I knew I would eventually get to a place where I felt better. I say I *knew;* the truth is, you never get to a place where you feel good about being a working mom (more on that in the Spotlight on Reshma Saujani in Chapter 8).

Advocating for yourself means advocating for your abilities and for your willingness to work. One thing that helped me get hired was my soft skills—I was easy to work with, and easy to teach. I was quick to learn, energetic, and enthusiastic. I showed up to *work* each day because what I was doing was aligned with my purpose.

I encourage you: Don't hold yourself back because you don't know how to do something. Be willing to learn, because if you have a willingness to learn you will succeed.

I recently was on set at QVC, and ten minutes before I was about to go live launching an innovative new product it hit me: I was realizing a dream years in the making. Just a few years prior, I dared to dream that one day I would be on television. I became an editor somewhat out of necessity, but I continued as an editor because the job enabled me to reach people. As I moved from job to job, I gained clarity on my mission in this life—to share useful information and tell compelling stories.

You might ask, "What does being on QVC have to do with that—it's just a sales tool." I would argue that it's more than that. Sure, the goal is to drive sales and make money, but for the hosts and product creators, it's about spreading a message and sharing useful information. Walking onto the set for the first time was a thrill. What once felt like an impossibility was now a reality.

Spotlight: Christine Michel Carter

Christine Michel Carter is a fierce advocate for working moms and the author of *Mom AF.*

In this excerpt from *The Breakdown with Bethany*, we talk about summit syndrome and how moms can advocate for themselves at work.

Bethany: We all know what imposter syndrome is, but you also talk about something called *summit syndrome*, which I find fascinating. Can you tell us a little bit about that?

Christine: Sure. I didn't coin that term—that was Robert Rose with the Content Marketing Institute. But it's imposter syndrome untreated. Women and minorities, folks who don't feel a sense of ambient belonging, who feel a disconnection in the workplace—they're the ones most likely to experience imposter syndrome.

Summit syndrome is the act of chasing an unattainable corporate high. I see it so many times with women who're saying, "Oh, I don't belong in the workplace, so let me go get my MBA. Let me go get three other master's degrees that have nothing to do with my function, and let me go get a bunch of certificates and start working on board memberships." They're accelerating burnout because they feel like they don't belong and they're trying to prove themselves.

Bethany: Yeah, you're really striking a nerve with me, because when I got into writing, editing, and digital publishing, I had absolutely no background as far as my education went, and I think that my imposter syndrome became summit syndrome. So, to hear it named makes me feel like I can take a deep breath.

Christine: Here's an interesting fact I usually share with companies: six out of ten people feel like imposters in their workplace. If you put that into perspective, at work or on social media, anytime you see ten people, *six* of them feel the same way you do. So, we're all battling imposter syndrome on one level or another, and there are many people who are trying to negate that with summit syndrome.

Bethany: Right. I also want to talk about something that I think a lot of working moms deal with. Of course, from the top down we often feel like we're not supported at work, either by our corporations or our bosses. But what about our counterparts, the people adjacent to us who have similar roles—coworkers or colleagues, even other women who may or may not be mothers? Can you give us your thoughts about that?

Christine: I just did a piece for *Forbes Women* about toxic femininity, and you would be surprised. When it comes to women of color, for example, the

> group that is most likely to help them with their careers and serve as mentors is white men. The last to help are white women. It's all in the article. And I completely get what you're saying—there are so many people who judge mothers for leaving early, and some of them are mothers themselves or women themselves. What folks don't realize is that they might be in that position one day—if not as a parent, then perhaps as a caregiver.
>
> Because we all are caregivers in some capacity in our lives, for kids or aging parents or older aunts or neighbors. The chances of someone in America being a caregiver are quite high. When you judge somebody for leaving early, or you don't help that person advance their career because you think that working parents aren't as dedicated or productive—which studies show is not the case—then you're ultimately hurting yourself when you end up in the same position.

To hear more of our interview, listen to Episode #16 of *The Breakdown with Bethany*.

Meet the Rule Breaker: Bozoma Saint John

Bozoma Saint John is a self-proclaimed badass. She's a mother and an executive marketer for companies like Apple Music, Pepsi, Uber, and most recently, Netflix.

Here are a few inspiring quotes from Bozoma on living out loud.

On Instagram (@badassboz) on March 7, 2022, Ghanaian Independence Day:[1]

"I'm free in every sense . . . physically, emotionally, and mentally. That is my super power. I've fought hard for it and believe me when I say it's still a daily struggle to maintain my freedom. Especially when the world tries to make me feel like I have to shift and change to fit into somebody else's standard. I refuse to bow down because my very being is in active revolt, so I expand."

In a March 2022 *Hollywood Reporter* interview after leaving Netflix:[2]

Here's the thing: I live out loud. I recognize that there are not a lot of Black women who are in these positions [chief marketing officer at Netflix]. Do I wish that sometimes I could be "just like everyone else"? Of course, who doesn't want to be? But the truth of the matter is, I'm not. In these spaces, there's nothing about me that is like anybody else. I recognize that I'm going to be talked about and sometimes I'm going to be talked about negatively because there's not an understanding of where I'm coming from, the culture I represent, the ways that I am. And those things feel like friction.

My hope now is that there are more of us who are different. And, by the way, that doesn't just apply to Black women. It applies to everybody. I think everybody's wearing a mask, figuratively, so I wish more of us would be able to [take it off] and really be exactly who we are. That way, I wouldn't seem so strange and so *other*.

Tips to Implement Right Now

1. Don't let a lack of education or professional experience hold you back.
2. Don't hesitate to apply for jobs you want, even if you don't meet 100% of the qualifications.
3. Advocate for yourself. In the workplace, act the way you want to be treated.

Recognize	**Reframe**	**Reconnect**
Take some time to ask yourself, "What do I want in life? What are my passions?"	If you haven't been moving toward your purpose, there is no better time to start than the present. Once you know your passions and understand your purpose, you can start pursuing them.	Start moving toward your goals. Encourage yourself by saying, "You can do this. You are worthy." Then, enlist the resources you need to help you move along.

Bethany's Chapter Breakdown

Advocate for yourself because in doing so, you are advocating for others.

CHAPTER 8:

Raising the Bar and Your Kids

"For me, being a mother made me a better professional, because coming home every night to my girls reminded me what I was working for. And being a professional made me a better mother, because by pursuing my dreams, I was modeling for my girls how to pursue their dreams.'"

-Michelle Obama

Old Rule: You can't raise a family and nurture a career at the same time.
New Rule: Your life can be crafted in any way you like, but be sure to enlist support.

For many years, I suffered pretty badly from imposter syndrome. And I don't think my imposter syndrome came out of an untrue place—I *was* somewhat of an imposter. I had a natural ability to write, but (as I've mentioned already) I had no formal training. I held myself back; I cowered down. I tried to be confident, but deep inside I was suffering, because there were things I didn't know, skills I hadn't learned. And I didn't know what I didn't know, which made things even worse.

On top of all that, I was a mother raising two young kids, so I needed flexibility. I couldn't always stay beyond 5 p.m. Some days I couldn't stay past 2 p.m. And on other days, I couldn't even make it into the office—and I *had* reliable childcare. Yet, I frequently needed to work from home, whether it was because I had a sick kid, was sick myself, or just felt like that's where I needed to be. Believe me, that didn't garner much support from my coworkers.

But in tandem with these difficulties, I also had a burning desire to achieve—and achieve at a high level. I'm not sure if my ambition was born out of the feeling that people didn't think I belonged in that world or if it was deep inside me and I discovered it as I discovered my passion for journalism. I felt unstoppable.

But I needed help. There's no doubt in my mind that I would not have achieved what I did without the help of my parents and my mother-in-law. My mother-in-law dropped everything to help me raise Elias in those first few years and did it again when I had my second son, Jake. I feel like my mother set me up with the mindset to succeed and my mother-in-law provided the support I needed in order to do so.

I was grateful to them both, but at the same time, I felt incredibly guilty about needing them. I felt so indebted. Their sacrifices enabled me to achieve my dreams, but I often felt unworthy. "I should be able to do this on my own," I thought. "I'm leaning on my family too much." These thoughts raced through my head regularly. It was only when I realized that the alternative was to kiss my dreams goodbye that I started to appreciate their time and help as a gift instead of feeling guilty about it.

I'm going to sidetrack here for a minute and talk about my mother-in-law, Margie. As I mentioned above, it was her love and dedication to her grandchildren that helped me feel safe and secure enough to chase after my ambitions. This is what loving *like a mother* is truly all about. Margie represents a selfless kind of love for which I will be forever grateful.

She passed in 2019, and things have never been quite the same. I don't expect that things will ever be the same. She showed me the power of a mother's love, and although the selflessness of Margie's love might seem contradictory to the message of this book, her love for her family was reflected in the love she had for herself. She and her family were one and the same. If there's one person I aim to love like, it's Margie. Her love kept us afloat, and we miss her every day.

I think a lot of women are at the top of their game when they decide to have children, already well up the corporate ladder. It seems like there should be a certain level of respect and understanding for those women. But is there? I've heard about women that have gone back to work *way* sooner than they should have because they feared losing their place at work.

I was one of them. I started a new job four weeks after having my second child via an emergency C-section. I was afraid to extend my start date because I didn't want to lose the job. They didn't have a pumping room for me, and I was afraid to ask for one, so I was leaking at work. Nobody understood; many of the women there weren't moms. It was such a challenge to balance it all. I was at the bottom of the totem pole with two kids, asking for flexibility, desperately trying to climb my way up, and getting dirty looks along the way.

If I could talk to myself back then—or better yet, give advice to another woman who is starting out on her career path—I would say, *ask* for those things—time off, a pumping room, and flexibility. In many cases, they are your legal right. It took me a long time to understand the power of using my own voice. When women use their voices, it changes the working dynamic.

Working and raising kids was already challenging prior to the pandemic. Two years later, millions of women have left the workforce. What does the path for working mothers look like now?

When the pandemic started, I was the head of Parenting.com, one of the top parenting websites in the country. After working there as an editor, I had taken the helm in February 2020, only to have the pandemic hit a month later. I spent the next year working furiously from my kitchen and running between bedrooms to get my kids onto virtual learning. At the time, I had one son in second grade and another in pre-K.

Like many working mothers, I felt completely unsupported. The system wasn't set up to support working mothers. I probably would have been better off mentally and physically if I had quit my job. But I was excited about my new position—I finally had a job leading a parenting site for one of the best publishers in the world. How could I leave?

But what happened was, my kids suffered, and I suffered—it was a shit show. I burned myself out of that job because what I was doing was unsustainable. And that messed me up for any job I had afterward.

I think many women had similar experiences. We were all trying to pivot and shift, trying to figure out what would work for us. But we couldn't make it work in a system that didn't support us.

After I left Parenting.com, I jumped around a lot. I worked at some other amazing

companies, but I didn't stay anywhere very long. I had burned myself out to the point where I wasn't doing well in any job in this industry that I love. So, I had to take a break and figure out what I wanted. I needed to recognize and reframe so I could reemerge with more power, ownership, and control over what I wanted my career and my life to look like.

I'm seeing this happen with many women. We're reemerging, coming back from a break we didn't want to take. My husband is a detective with the NYPD, and sometimes he says he's not *volunteered* but "voluntold" to work overtime. Optional overtime, but not really. The setbacks for women during the pandemic were like that. We took the hit; we forgot our careers to take care of our families. Now that things are going back to normal, what will normal look like? How are we going to shape it? Are we going to create new rules, our own rules, so that *maybe* this doesn't happen again?

What happened to women during the pandemic was devastating. We have to think about what's next. We have the power to shape the future however we want to. In a sense, that's the main idea of this book. As women are reemerging into the workforce, and into society, we're coming with our own rules in hand, and we need to help each other enforce them.

Maybe you're still stuck in the pandemic fog, feeling defeated and beaten down. Maybe you lost your business during the pandemic, or you've started a new one that hasn't gotten off the ground yet. Let me encourage you.

First, recognize what's going on. Take a second to understand why you're struggling. I had to stop and figure out why I was failing in an industry I had worked so hard to reach the top of. I needed to recognize that I was unhappy because of things that happened during the pandemic.

After you recognize, reframe. I had to reframe, to figure out how I was going to shift. I still want to be in the media, and I still want to be an editor, but I have to make it work for me. I have to reframe it; I might have to let some things go.

Third, reconnect. I had to reconnect with why I love what I do. I had to reconnect with my

family and figure out the balance once again because that's a constant battle.

After you recognize, reframe, and reconnect, you're ready to reemerge. I was able to come back stronger, but it took a lot of time. Actually, I tried to reemerge three or four times, but I did it in ways that didn't work. So, I had to go back and reflect and figure it out.

What will your reemergence look like? Think about the best version of yourself and envision it out there in the world. Start working toward that vision every day, and don't be afraid to try and try again if it doesn't work out. Choose yourself time and time again.

Spotlight: Reshma Saujani

Reshma Saujani is an author and the founder of Girls Who Code and Moms First (formerly Marshall Plan for Moms).

The thoughts, feelings, fears, hopes, and demands that I've only ever dreamed of— Reshma trumpets them for the world to hear. Mothers have been struggling for a long time, and with someone like her at the helm of Moms First, it feels like change is coming like we have a bit of hope. I'm proud to have her speak on behalf of me and other working mothers.

Here's part of our conversation on the shared identity (and power) of mothers.

Bethany: How would you describe the current landscape of working motherhood in the US?

Reshma: I think that for far too long, America has undervalued its mothers. Our nation's childcare is in crisis—40% of parents are in debt because of pre-K. The cost of childcare is rising faster than the rate of inflation.

Half of the daycare centers are still shut down. We're the only industrialized nation that doesn't have paid leave. The vast majority of moms go back to work too soon after having a baby. Anytime I speak at a conference, I ask that question: "How many of you went back to work too early, and it scarred you?" Every hand is raised. We have impossible cultural expectations on mothers, so that whatever choices they make seem like they're the wrong ones. And while society is kind of minimizing our challenges and devaluing our joy, it's flattening our messy contradictions rather than holding space for them.

Here's the best case scenario: I want to create a society where women have the freedom to move in and out of the workforce without penalty, where there's truly a sense of freedom and choice. That's something we just don't have—it's constantly one or the other.

A Pew study came out a couple days ago about how parents are (1) more unhappy, and (2) feel like they're under higher expectations than our parents were. We are doing more than single mothers did in the 1970s.

All that is a consequence, I think, of the high-hustle culture we have in workplaces and the intensive parenting we have because of social media. And it's just crashing. And mothers are the carnage of that. We need to have a radically different conversation today than we've ever had.

Bethany: Yeah, I feel that so, so deeply. One thing you've talked about before is the shared identity we have as mothers and the power of that. Can you talk to us about what that means, what kind of power we hold, and how we don't realize it yet?

Reshma: Yeah. In a sense, this is where the pandemic was a gift. The pandemic showed us that we have a shared identity. I think what was happening pre-pandemic—I'll illustrate with my own marriage. I was running one of the largest women and girls' organizations in the world, Girls Who Code, struggling with fertility, having kids. And I married a good guy, you know? But still, I was doing more of the housework and more of that "untenable balance." And I kept thinking, "This is my fault. I haven't trained him well enough." It was my private, hell—everybody else had things figured out, because they look so damn happy. And then the pandemic hits and I was like, "Oh... no, we've

> all been lying." We've all been lying about our lives, whether we're Black or brown, poor, or rich, straight or gay. And we're all mothers, so there's a sense of commonality or shared experience in the way we're experiencing personal life, professional life, and society. So, in a way, the pandemic opened up a massive opportunity to create a motherhood identity.
>
> For Moms First, one of our taglines is "Putting motherhood before party." I'm excited to build an apolitical, bipartisan community where we can become *childcare* voters, where we can actually build off of our common sense that we're all getting fucked. That's the opportunity right now.

To hear more of our interview, listen to Episode #18 of The Breakdown with Bethany.

Meet the Rule Breaker: Jacinda Ardern

It was hard to turn on the news in the last few years without hearing or seeing something about former New Zealand Prime Minister Jacinda Ardern. She made headlines for the way she led, the way she mothered, becoming only the second head of state to give birth to a baby while in office, and, ultimately, the way she resigned.

To me, Ardern was more than the leader of a nation—she represented much-needed change. From banning assault rifles to embracing empathy and morality, Ardern led with strength and heart, just like a mother.

Here's a bit of what Jacinda Ardern has said about how to lead.

In a December 2019 interview with *Newshub*, on how motherhood affected her leadership:1 To me, leadership is not about necessarily being the loudest in the room, but instead being the bridge, or the thing that is missing in the discussion and trying to build a consensus from there I guess that can somewhat be applied to mother, as you are constantly doing whatever it is that your little one needs at that particular moment.

In August 2017, a day after taking the leadership of New Zealand's Labour Party (prior to being elected prime minister), Ardern was asked whether it would be okay for a woman to take maternity leave while serving as prime minister. She responded:[2]

It is totally unacceptable in 2017 to say that women should have to answer that question in the workplace. It is unacceptable It is a woman's decision about when they choose to have children, and it should not predetermine whether or not they are given a job or have job opportunities.

Tips to Implement Right Now

1. Visit MomsFirst.us, the organization founded by Reshma Saujani for a host of resources to help you along your working-mom journey.
2. Talk to other working moms. Having open and honest conversations about salary, flexibility, and childcare helps destigmatize these things in the workplace and empowers you to ask for what you deserve.
3. Ask for help—from your partner, parents, friends, and community. Work and motherhood are hard, but they

don't have to be lonely. Enlist your community for support, and don't be afraid to let certain things go (see ya, housework!).

Bethany's Chapter Breakdown

Ask for help. Demand it if you must.

CHAPTER 9:

Mentors and Community

"A mentor is someone who allows you to see the hope inside yourself."

-Oprah Winfrey

Old Rule: A mentor is nice to have but not vital to your success.
New Rule: Gather as many mentors as you can, even if you don't know them personally.

If anyone ever needed a mentor, it was me from 2012–2017. I had drive and passion but not direction. I made embarrassing mistakes, faltered, fell, screamed and cried (at home *and* in the office bathroom), and felt hopeless many, many times. Still, I kept working, climbing my way up, carving out a space for myself despite feeling utterly alone.

I craved mentorship. Maybe it was the only child in me, longing to be seen, understood, and supported by a peer, and there were many times when I wanted guidance from someone with more experience. But here's the thing—I didn't get that guidance until I started actively seeking it out.

Since 2017, I have been greatly helped by mentors. It's not surprising that they've mostly been women. What *is* surprising is that I only know a few of them personally. I found mentors who had no idea I existed. Secret mentors, if you will, that I followed on social media, learned from, and studied what they were putting out there. I dug into their history and how they got to where they were.

One of the mentors I found was Joelle Garguilo. I saw her on NBC's local lifestyle show *New York Live*, and I was really struck by her energy. I thought, "This woman's amazing. She's a mom, she has so much energy, and she's so fun." You can really see her passion for what she was doing shine through (and you still can). I followed her on Instagram and started commenting and liking and watching what she did. Unbeknownst to me was that Joelle made a major pivot to working in media. She started in accounting and decided that she wanted to be a reporter. And she did it—I watched so much of her journey from the sidelines but took in everything I could along the way. Sidenote, if you don't know Joelle, look her up, she's one of the best interviewers in the business.

I thought, "If I'm going to pivot from editing to being on camera, *I've* got to learn all the ins and outs of the business." So, I followed Joelle. I wanted to be just like her. I learned so many lessons watching her—I took in things I saw her doing without Joelle even knowing I existed. She had no idea who I was.

Finally, in 2021—after sending her many pitches—I got on-air with Joelle on New York Live, and we did a segment together, the very same show I studied her on so many years ago. Since then, we've developed a great friendship—we do things together, we hang out.

It's still shocking to me. She even wrote the foreword to this book! Joelle is inspiring not only in how she shows up professionally but also in how she supports and continues to support people (like me) personally. How we show up matters—for ourselves and for others. Be like Joelle!

My point here is to cultivate your own community. There are ways to cultivate community without going out there and shaking hands, introducing yourself, and launching into your elevator pitch. You can cultivate community from your bedroom. The right people will find you. Joelle will tell you that she's not my mentor and that we're friends, but she is. She is one of my biggest mentors, and I was able to cultivate that for myself because of how much I admired her and still do. Like the quote from Oprah at the beginning of the chapter states, watching and learning from Joelle allowed me to see the hope inside myself. Find someone that does that for you, it will be the best thing you ever do!

Spotlight: Stephanie Cartin

Stephanie Cartin is a serial entrepreneur and co-founder of Entreprenista, Socialfly, and The Entreprenista League, an amazing professional community. I jumped when I was given the opportunity to join!

I met Steph when she invited me to be on Entreprenista, the podcast she hosts with her business partner, Courtney Spritzer. We clicked right away over our shared ambition and love of the red heart emoji. I believe in Steph's vision of "elevating women through community."

Steph and I chatted about the importance of community and mentors.

Bethany: Something that has really helped me is mentors. And many of the mentors I've had, I didn't even know them personally. I just watched them, emulated them, and learned from their drive and example. Do you have any stories of mentorship that you've seen within The Entreprenista League or from your own personal experience?

Stephanie: Yes. I love sharing this story. I get the chills even thinking about it. When Courtney and I started Socialfly, we were introduced to a woman named Carrie Kerpen. She also runs a social media agency. We were introduced to her very early on in our business.

Courtney and I were in our early and mid-twenties, super young in business. And we met with Carrie and she was like, "Ladies, I love what you're doing. I was in your shoes. I want to help you. I want to support you." And she became one of our best friends and mentors in business to this day. We literally were in the exact same business; we were just a few years behind. And she was referring clients to us, helping us. She wanted to support us because there is enough business to go around for everyone. We don't need to be so competitive with each other. We can all support and coach each other and be there to lift each other up. And Carrie was a true example of that for us.

Courtney and I learned from that, and we have now mentored and supported so many other women a few years behind us in business, especially in agency businesses. Several years ago, I connected with a woman on Instagram named Katie Love. She's now part of The Entreprenista League. We became fast friends and Courtney and I started to mentor her. And we've been able to refer business to her and help her grow her business. Because, as I said, we can all help each other. There's enough business out there for everyone. These kinds of connections are happening literally every day in our community.

Bethany: I think that's a really important mindset to have. Because honestly, I think women feel pitted against each other sometimes. Or because we're working so hard, because we're navigating family life or being underpaid, we feel like there's not enough. But we can come from a mindset that there *is* enough, and if we're going up, we can reach behind to grab other people and lift them up.

Stephanie: Community and connection is everything. Don't try to do everything alone. Don't feel like you have to do everything yourself. There are communities available, people that want to support and help. So don't be scared to reach out and ask for help. If you're thinking about starting a business, and it's something you've

> thought about for a long time and you really want to do it but you're holding back, my best piece of advice is to just *start.* Just get started and surround yourself with people who have done it before. They will help you if you just reach out to ask. So just get started.

To hear more of our interview, listen to Episode #33 of *The Breakdown with Bethany.*

Meet the Rule Breaker: Shellye Archambeau

Shellye Archambeau is a veteran Board Director and the former CEO of MetricStream. She is currently a Board Director at Verizon, Roper Technologies, and Okta. She has spent the bulk of her career helping others achieve their goals and created a community around her ideas on mentorship.

Here's what Shellye had to say about mentors in her book, *Unapologetically Ambitious.*1

> There's an interesting dynamic that develops between mentors and mentees. As a mentee, when you first meet someone whose brain you want to pick, you may not know much about their personality. Your instinct tells you to do whatever they suggest. But the point of mentorship isn't to serve someone more successful than yourself; it's to ask them to serve you, in their own way.
>
> I believe that almost all people truly want to help, in their hearts. If you make it easy for them, and you make sure they see results, they feel wonderful about it.

Tips to Implement Right Now

1. Find mentors—ones who will actively mentor you or ones you can look to for inspiration. You don't have to know your mentor personally to be their mentee. Is there someone you relate to? Even if they are aspirational, find ways to reach out, and start acting as if they are already mentoring you.
2. Join a community. In 2022, I joined three different professional communities with the intention of meeting people, growing my network, and discovering new opportunities. If you crave a mentor, communities are the best place to start. Plus, you can straight up ask for mentorship, because communities like The Entreprenista League are so supportive.
3. Can't find a mentor? Be one. I've mentored several women over the years for short periods of time and each one taught me way more than I expected. Connecting with people who are younger than you can be a valuable lesson and keep you open to new experiences.

Recognize	Reframe	Reconnect
Feeling lost or feeling like you need guidance is a strong indication that you could be helped by a mentor.	Shift your thinking from "I feel lost" to "I know there are people out there that can help me." You can seek out mentors without knowing them personally and even without asking them to mentor you. Study them. What do they wake up inside of you? What is it that you admire about them? Start making small shifts.	Once you've identified a mentor, emulate what they do. Figure out the best way to approach them- perhaps by complimenting their recent work, asking if they are open to having a mentee, or connecting on LinkedIn. Turn your small shifts into bigger ones, and remember to keep learning. Never stop absorbing lessons. If you can learn, you can succeed.

Bethany's Chapter Breakdown

Choose who you want as a mentor and make it easy for them to mentor you.

CHAPTER 10:

Shoot for the Stars

"Start before you're ready. Don't prepare, begin."
-Mel Robbins

It's hard to start. But the great thing about starting is that you can do it at any time, and you can do it over and over again.

Although we're coming to the end of this book, the journey is far from over. In fact, this is just the beginning—or at least I hope it is. I hope you take the tips, insight, and advice from the women featured in this book and launch out into the world. But more importantly, I hope you take it into yourself and use it to create the best life you can.

I toyed with different titles for this book, and one candidate that nearly made the cut was *First Comes Love*. We—especially little girls—learn the nursery rhyme so young, and it's ingrained in us: "First comes love, then comes marriage, then comes the baby in the baby carriage." As I was growing and creating my own life, carving out my own path, blazing my own trail, I realized that there are many things like this ingrained in us—ways we're supposed to be and look, ways we're supposed to talk and feel, or how to order our lives, the timeline. It's all bullshit. I thought about calling this book *First Comes Love* to take the old nursery rhyme and turn it on its head.

No matter what you do—no matter what career you choose or how you decide to raise (or not raise) a family, whether you choose to be married or single—we have to love ourselves first. That's the most important thing. The title *Like a Mother* won out because it is so reflective of where I am *now*. I live and show up every day like a mother—with love, tenacity, fierceness, and empathy.

Now, it's your turn. Whether your next steps are small or big, I hope I've encouraged you to write your own rules for your life so you can reemerge to be your happiest and most fulfilled self.

The Like a Mother Journal

When I finish a book, I often wonder, "Well, what do I do now?"

What's your next step? Maybe it's something tangible, like applying for a job, going after a small business loan, or writing a book. Maybe it's something intangible, like a mindset shift—shifting the way you show up in your relationships with your family and friends, carving out more time for yourself, or making yourself a priority.

In digital media we use a metric called **bounce rate**, which measures how long someone stays on a specific web page before they leave. The goal is to have a low bounce rate; you want people to stay and look around your site.

Well, I don't want you to bounce. I don't want you to have to set this book aside to search for your next steps. You can start right here. We take the best action immediately after we're inspired. So, if you were inspired, don't leave—stay and write.

I've set up this chapter for you to use as a journal, complete with a review of what we've covered and prompts to stimulate your thoughts. Your **Like a Mother** Journal can be your blueprint and launch your journey to banish guilt, blaze your trail, and break the rules to create a life you love.

Part 1: Let's Talk About Self, Baby!

How do you talk about yourself?
*In Part 1, we broke down all things **you**—*
how you love yourself, talk to yourself, and
blaze your trail. What comes to mind when
you're asked about these three things?

Chapter 1: Self-Love

New Rule: *Put yourself first unapologetically and be loud about it.*

Do you start your day with self-love? How do you love yourself in the first moments after you wake up?

Make a self-love contract. What will your morning self-love ritual look like? When will you start? Write down a specific date!

Chapter 2: Self-Talk

New Rule: You are your own best friend, so start talking to yourself like it.

What would you like to say to yourself? What do your friends love about you? Write down everything that makes you incredible.

What do you say to your friends when they are feeling down? Write it down as a letter to yourself.

Chapter 3: Bet on Yourself

New Rule: Create your own opportunities and remember that you are limitless. What is your BIG dream? What would you do if you couldn't fail?

What is holding you back?

What can you do today that's different? How can you start blazing your trail?

Part 2: Friends, Lovers, and Others

Think about how you relate to others. How can you start putting yourself first? Think about your closest and most meaningful relationships and how you can make them better.

Chapter 4: I Now Denounce You

New Rule: *Continue to put yourself first, even in relationships.*

Where are you giving too much away in your relationships? How can you start getting it back?

What do you want to say to your spouse/partner? Write it here first (trust me on that!).

Chapter 5: Boundaries Can Be a Real Bitch

New Rule: The most successful relationships have boundaries. It's often with the people we love the most that boundaries are required.

What boundaries do you want to set?

Write a script for setting boundaries with loved ones.

What are your boundary triggers? Write down how you plan to reset your boundaries if they're crossed.

Chapter 6: Roots and Wings

New Rule: *Honor yourself and own your individuality. In your life right now, what's working, what's not working, and what change do you plan to make?*

What attributes make you unique?

What do you want to forgive yourself for so you can move forward?

Part 3: Work and Ambition

Ambition is **not** *a dirty word, and there's simply no space for guilt around trying to achieve high standards in our careers. But we do need support. Think about how you can support yourself in your ambitions and what you need from others in the way of support.*

Chapter 7: Working Girl

New Rule: Go for it and learn on the job. Do things in ways that work for you. What's your dream job? What are you passionate about? How can you start owning it?

How do you advocate for yourself?

What does "blazing your trail" look like to you?

Chapter 8: Raising the Bar and Your Kids

New Rule: Your life can be crafted in any way you like but be sure to enlist support. What help do you need right now? How are you going to get it?

What does accountability look like to you? How do you plan to keep others accountable? What's the first step to raising your own bar?

Chapter 9: Mentors and Community

New Rule: *Gather as many mentors as you can, even if you don't know them personally. Where do you struggle with making connections?*

Who is your ideal mentor? Write out your "Will you be my mentor?" script.

What does your ideal professional community look like? What steps do you plan to take to create your tribe?

Chapter 10: Shoot for the Stars

In this book, I've highlighted the attributes of 18 women. We've seen how they've broken the rules and made their own rules to live their best life.

Now, I believe you're ready to take impactful steps toward honoring yourself, breaking the rules, and living ***your*** *best life. So, here's a space for you to give yourself praise— to spotlight* ***yourself****.*

What did you learn about yourself as you read this book?

___

___

___

___

___

Write down something you're proud of, perhaps something you've never recognized before.

___

___

___

___

___

What else do you want to say about yourself?

___

___

___

___

Meet the Rule Breaker: The Future You

This chapter's rule breaker is . . . ***you!***

I hope this book has prepared you to jettison old rules that are holding you back or not contributing to your success and laid a foundation for you to create new rules that enable you to build a life you love!

What rules are you ready to break that aren't serving you any longer? What are your new rules for your life?

_________________'s new rules for self-love:

_________________'s new rules for navigating relationships:

_________________'s new rules for work and ambition:

The Final Breakdown

What's your final breakdown? If you had to sum up what you got out of this book in one impactful sentence, what would you write? Send it to me!

I'm proud of you! Not only so, I want to hear from you. If you've taken the time to read this book and fill out the journal prompts, please let me know. Maybe you're my next podcast guest or a Spotlight in my next book. Cultivating community has been such a boon to my personal and professional success. We need our village! Imagine what a village it would be if we were all blazing ahead with no guilt, operating by a set of rules we've written for ourselves. I think we can do it. I know we can!

Thank you for reading my book!

My mission is and will always be to help working moms live a life beyond their wildest dreams.

Here's how you can help me spread that message.

Let's Break It Down Together:

1. Leave a review on Amazon
   Book reviews help books reach readers. Leave a review, letting everyone know what you thought of the book.
2. Listen to the podcast
   Download The Breakdown With Bethany on Apple Podcasts or Spotify. If you think you would make a great guest email me at bethany@thebreakdownwithbethany.com
3. Share the book with a friend
   Word of mouth is everything! If you enjoyed this book, please tell another woman you love.
4. Subscribe to The Breakdown With Bethany Newsletter
   Stay up to date on everything that's happening with the podcast, events I'm hosting, and ways we can work together. Head over to my website: bethany@bethanybraunsilva.com to subscribe.
5. Work with me
   I am a public speaker, coach, writer, and editor! If you would like to work with me, please contact me at bethany@bethanybraunsilva.com

Join our community at:

https://likeamotherbook.com/

ACKNOWLEDGMENTS

Writing this book has been a dream of mine for a long time, and I have so many people to thank.

Thank you to:

My mother for the endless inspiration.

My father for being the most empathic person on the planet and the best listener.

Manny, for being my eternal boyfriend.

My children, Elias and Jake. Thank you for teaching me what true love is all about.

My girls, Julia, Kim, Delilah, and Brandi; thank you for being my emotional safety net for literal decades.

Margie, for being the ultimate example of what loving "Like a Mother" truly is.

Lisa, for being the sister I always dreamed of.

Danielle and Joelle, for being the best new friends.

All the amazing women who have appeared on The Breakdown With Bethany to tell their stories with the hope of inspiring others.

Cheli, for helping me put it all together.

And to all the mothers everywhere, I see you, I am you, I love you.

END NOTES

Introduction

1. Stacey Vanek Smith, "Women, work and the pandemic," NPR, June 9, 2021, https://www.npr.org/2021/06/09/1004892039/women-work-and-the-pandemic

Chapter 2

1. "Internal dialogue or self-talk," College of Cognitive Behavioural Therapies, accessed April 27, 2023, https://www.cbttherapies.org.uk/2014/07/28/internal-dialogue-self-talk/
2. Isabel González Whitaker, "J. Lo's flying high," *Harper's Bazaar*, March 15, 2018, https://www.harpersbazaar.com/culture/features/a19181340/jennifer-lopez interview-2018/.

Chapter 3

1. Sheryl Sandberg, *Lean In: Women, Work, and the Will to Lead* (New York: Alfred A. Knopf, 2013).
2. Sheryl Sandberg, "Why we have too few women leaders," TED (video), accessed April 27, 2023, https://www.ted.com/talks/sheryl_sandberg_why_we_have_too_few_women_leaders.
3. Keke Palmer, *I Don't Belong to You: Quiet the Noise and Find Your Voice*, trade paperback edition (New York: Gallery Books, 2019), 16.

Chapter 4

1. Gabby Bernstein, "Practice the choose again method to shift out of negative thoughts and feel better," Gabby (website), September 19, 2019, https://gabbybernstein.com/choose again/.
2. Tara Schuster, *Buy Yourself the F*cking Lilies: And Other Rituals to Fix Your Life, from Someone Who's Been There* (New York: The Dial Press, 2019), 317.

Chapter 5

1. Glennon Doyle, *Untamed* (New York: The Dial Press, 2020), 267.

Chapter 6

1. "Prince William, Kate Middleton, Prince Harry & Meghan Markle discuss the Royal Foundation," @braxsquad, YouTube (video), accessed April 27, 2023, https://youtu.be/t0IF9iT91Ek.
2. Allison P. Davis, "Meghan the Duchess," *The Cut*, August 29, 2022, https://www.thecut.com/article/meghan-markle-profile-interview.html.

Chapter 7

1. Bozoma Saint John (@badassboz), Instagram post, March 7, 2022, https://www.instagram.com/p/Cazmu18oNv5/.
2. Chris Gardner, "Bozoma Saint John talks Netflix exit, responds to criticism about her personal brand: 'I Live Out Loud'," *The Hollywood Reporter*, March 22, 2022, https://www.hollywoodreporter.com/tv/tv-news/bozoma-saint-john-interview-netflix instagram-badass-boz-1235117060/.

Chapter 8

1. Jamie Ensor, "Mother's Day: Prime Minister Jacinda Ardern on motherhood influencing leadership," *Newshub*, December 5, 2019, https://www.newshub.co.nz/home/lifestyle/2019/05/mother-s-day-prime-minister-jacinda ardern-on-motherhood-influencing-leadership.html.
2. "Jacinda Ardern: NZ opposition leader hits back over baby questions," *BBC News*, August 2, 2017, https://www.bbc.com/news/world-asia-40798966.

Chapter 9

1. Shellye Archambeau, *Unapologetically Ambitious: Take Risks, Break Barriers, and Create Success on Your Own Terms* (New York: Grand Central Publishing, 2020), 236.

ABOUT THE AUTHOR

Bethany Braun-Silva is an on-air parenting, entertainment, and lifestyle expert and the host of "The Breakdown With Bethany" podcast and web show on Mom.com, where she interviews incredible women on topics like motherhood, work and ambition, self-care, and more. She is also an experienced digital editor, having helmed Parenting.com. Her writing has appeared in *People, Parents, Real Simple, Shape*, and more.

Photo: Michelle Rose